This is a great book that would enrich anyone's life!! An easy read that was very informative and entertaining.

–Pastor John F. Stocker Resurrection
Fellowship Loveland, CO (retired)

Flowers Whisper is a treasure that you can turn to again and again for hope and encouragement. Debbie's words are the paintbrush for God's beauty.

–Stephanie DeWayne co-founder Breast Friends
Breast Cancer Support Group Foundation

Debbie's generous heart speaks to all of us through the beauty of her stories in Flowers Whisper. They will touch your heart with God's love.

–Rev. Cheryl Smith

Your faith will blossom as you read Debbie's wonderful stories.

–Rev. Eldon Schmidt

About the Author

Debbie Martin has been in the floral business as a successful florist for over 30 years. A public speaker, business and personal mentor and author of *Flowers Whisper*, Debbie is dedicated to her faith, family and to serving others. Debbie's mission in life is to share her own life experiences and inspiring stories to enlighten, encourage and change other people's perspective on life and living.

Over the years, she has experienced some of life's greatest moments through her career and the journey of life. A walking miracle as a breast cancer survivor, Debbie co-founded Breast Friends Cancer Support Group Foundation Inc. As the Executive Director, she plants flowers of loving encouragement and seeds of faith empowering other breast cancer survivors to experience the joy of being a breast friend for a fellow "Breast Friend".

The power of love, giving love or expressing love is the greatest gift of all. Debbie believes we can add an enormous amount of value to other people's lives when we care, encourage and love them, lifting them up and helping them realize their own significance and worth. Through our words and actions, we show them how much they are valued. Debbie also believes that Jesus has a purpose and a plan for everything, as it will be done for the good of all. Her grateful living testimonies will enlighten, empower, strengthen and encourage anyone to live life to the fullest, with a deeper and more meaningful legacy.

Flowers Whisper

what words can't say...

Flowers Whisper

what words can't say...

Everyone needs a flower

Debbie Martin

Quantity discounts are available on bulk orders.
Contact sales@TAGPublishers.com for more information.

TAG Publishing, LLC
2618 S. Lipscomb
Amarillo, TX 79109
www.TAGPublishers.com

Office (806) 373-0114
Fax (806) 373-4004
info@TAGPublishers.com

ISBN: 978-1-59930-353-6

First Edition

Cover & Text: Lloyd Arbour, www.tablloyd.com

Dedication

I would like to dedicate this book to my loving family.

My husband, Kevin, who is my best friend, my companion, the one I laugh with, the one I cry with, my soul mate, and the one I love. As we celebrate 25 years of an incredible, wonderful marriage.

My daughter, Krystle, who is my friend and everything good, and everything beautiful. As God's gift, she touches my heart with kisses from heaven.

My son, Warren, who is positively inspiring, the power of strength and muscle - but always caring and giving. As God's gift sent from heaven, he brightens the world, touching my heart.

I would also like to dedicate this book to all of the family and friends who have blessed me with God's love and grace.

Acknowledgments

How can I possibly thank everyone who has touched my life? Words just don't seem to be enough to express the heartfelt appreciation for everything that everyone has done.

It is impossible to express adequate appreciation to those to whom this book is dedicated—my husband, Kevin, my daughter, Krystle, and my son, Warren—without whom this would not have been possible. You are the loves of my life. Thank you for all the sacrifices you've made and for all the support and encouragement throughout the journey of my life.

Thank you, Mom and Dad, Bob and Janet Winter, for encouraging and supporting me with faith at an early age, helping me to follow my dreams and pursue the joy in my life. Thank you for giving me the opportunity to share the wonderful years of the floral business experiences together. I am forever grateful for your love, encouragement, support, care, concern, and friendship. You are truly wonderful!

Thank you to my precious in-laws, Melvin and Nancy Martin, for your incredible son. I am forever grateful to you for raising the very wonderful man with whom I share my life. Thank you for always being there and for loving me like a daughter. You are so special, and I'm so blessed to have you as family.

This book would not be possible without TAG Publishing. I am so very grateful to Liz Ragland and Dee Burks for their friendship, their support, and their variety of professional services. Thank you for all your support for me as a first-time author and for the enormous amount of time, late nights, extended support, encouragement, prayers, wisdom, dedication, hard work, sacrifices, energy, and creative ideas you contributed.

To Stephanie DeWayne, co-founder of Breast Friends Cancer Support Group, and best friend. Thank you for the enormous amount of support, wardrobe consulting, faith, love, encouragement, friendship, prayer, sacrifices, wisdom, and counseling during my journey with cancer, the book, and in life. Thank you for sharing with such loyalty and dedication the passion and caring heart for our fellow sisters touched with breast cancer. You are someone whom I love dearly.

To Pam Jayne, my dear friend, for always being there. Thank you for your personal support, love, faith, and treasured friendship.

To Cathy Buchanan, fellow florist and dear friend. Thank you for your love, loyalty, friendship, energy, creativity, laughter, and hilarious wit, which have made life pure joy.

To Denise Wiedeman, fellow floral designer and dear friend. Thank you for your words of faith and for not fearing to answer my prayer in the decision to follow through with the book.

To Kim Martin, sister-in-law and friend. Thank you for sharing the inspiring mission, Touch of Faith, with me. Thank you for the years of support for me in the floral business and for sharing the same vision of the flowers touching lives with faith and caring for others. I am truly blessed to have you as family and friend.

To Julie Rothe, sister and dear friend. Thank you for all of your love and support over the years and for sewing all of my turbans and hats for me during my cancer journey. Thank you for all of your support starting the Stitches for Love campaign and for sewing the hair fashion, heart pillows and comforts for chemo victims.

To Tracy Morey, co-founder of Breast Friends Cancer Support Group, dear friend, supporter, and the inspiration to Bible Study Fellowship. Thank you for all of your love, faith, prayer, and encouragement.

Thank you to all of the women in Bible Study Fellowship for your continued prayers, faith, and support.

Thank you to all of the women of Breast Friends Cancer Support Group, the sisters who touch my life and my heart.

Thank you to Mark Shearon, PSI Seminars, Karen and Richard Roth, and everyone in PSI World for making a positive difference for one starfish at a time (like me). Thank you for inspiring me to write a book and make a difference.

To Michelle Kooi, thank you for all your help with editing and proofreading.

To Bonnie and Dave Tiffany, thank you for the words of faith, encouragement, support, and prayer; for being my hairdresser (even when I had no hair), and for your constant, treasured friendship throughout the years.

To Peggy Schlomer, my friend and nurse during chemo as well as her husband Marlin. Thank you both for all of your love, support, fundraising golf tournament, prayer, encouragement, and help in life. Thank you for sharing the passion of flowers.

To Juanita Stites, my floral broker during my entire floral career, for being my best friend. Thank you with all of my heart for who you are and for everything you do.

To Ken Kisselman, my loyal friend, teacher, and inspiration to write the stories of what flowers do for people. Thank you for your loyal support; I cherish your friendship. With more practice, I will get it right one of these days.

Thank you to my loving family, Rob and Becky Winter, Jason and Julie Rothe, Loren and Kim Martin, Wes Martin from New York, and Clark Schaneman. Thank you to all of my aunts, uncles, parents, grandparents, and cousins, for all of your love and support over the years and through the journey in the garden of life.

A book like this could not be written without the lives of others influencing its impact with their heartfelt life stories. Thank you to the clients and customers who have touched my life over the years through the floral business. You have each been a significant flower in my garden and have enriched my life beyond measure! You have touched my heart more than words can say.

Finally, it is impossible for me to list the names of everyone who so greatly deserves to be acknowledged for the influence you have had in my life. I should write a book of gratitude for everyone in my life. I know your name, it is written in my heart.

Thank you to all of the friends who have become like the family along the way. Thank you to all of the loving church family of Faith, as we are all friends in Christ. Thank you to the community of Windsor for all your love, loyalty, friendships, and support for the Breast Friends Cancer Support Group and for this first book, *Flowers Whisper*.

Contents

Introduction

Flowers are one of the greatest gifts to give and to receive. They appeal to all of our senses and brighten up our lives and our hearts. Flowers bring good cheer and convey the right message in their own language—the truest language of love for people of any age. I'm so captivated by the power of flowers in a child, teen, man or woman.

All over the world there are many traditions, beliefs, poems, and stories that glorify the beauty and uniqueness of flowers. Flowers are present during all of life's beautiful moments and are always there to share in our happiness. From life's simplest moments to its grandest, flowers make these times more meaningful and worth celebrating. I have a fabulous job because I get to spread love around the world in the form of flowers.

Flowers tell us how wonderful our life is meant to be, which is why I wrote *Flowers Whisper*. Perhaps you find it difficult to share your feelings in words, but you can express your exact sentiments by presenting flowers. *Flowers Whisper* is sprinkled with stories that will change your perspective of flowers and impact your life. Take the time to get involved with each and every story. Be aware of your emotions and feelings as the stories touch the depths of the soul. Some stories will speak louder to you than others.

Some might have a deeper meaning or make you think of someone special. There is no right or wrong reaction; what matters is that you are moved in some way. It is my wish to share with you through this book how flowers have touched my life, and I hope that with each turn of the page, they'll touch your life too.

Chapter 1
The Circle of Life

One of my favorite quotes is by Lydia M. Child: "Flowers have spoken to me more than I can tell in written words. They are the hieroglyphics of angels, loved by all men for the beauty of their character, though few can decipher even fragments of their meaning."

As Lydia states above, flowers have also whispered to me more than I can read in a book as well. In my career as a florist, I am blessed to spend my time working with one of God's greatest gifts—flowers. Over the years, I have grown to appreciate flowers to a greater extent as I experience their wonder and the beauty they bring to the world around us.

Flowers affect people in many different ways when they are given or received, and I have had the pleasure of witnessing this miracle from both perspectives. As each experience unfolds, a person begins to wonder how many people have really been touched by the joy that giving and receiving flowers can bring.

It is amazing that when you ask people when they last received flowers they know the answer faster than their tongue can speak. They can probably tell you the number of times they have received flowers, and chances are they can count them on one hand. As the individual starts to share the story of when they received a bouquet of flowers, their personality becomes charged with positive energy. They will then be able to share the date they received the flowers, who sent them, what they were for, what kind they were, and how much it meant to be surprised with something as simple as a flower.

Flowers are given in times of both joy and sorrow and are an extension of our feelings - love, admiration, get-well wishes, congratulations, appreciation, comfort, friendship, excitement, apology, and forgiveness. Flowers are always the best way to convey our emotions to another person because they are always appropriate! Flowers help to define a moment and will be enjoyed and remembered long after the moment is gone.

The language of flowers is quite extensive and can be easily understood no matter what native language an individual speaks. The flowers are silent, yet they can speak words in any moment: "I love you", "I'm sorry", "Good luck", "Congratulations", "Best wishes," "Get well soon," "My deepest sympathy and condolences," and "You're the best." What else can say all of that and *more* in every language around the globe? Flowers are linguistic geniuses.

You can hand flowers to any person on any continent, and they will appreciate and understand what you are saying. At one time or another, almost everyone has experienced the indescribable joy of receiving flowers. Everyone, both men and women, with whom I've talked have described the gift of flowers to be unlike any other. Why? The answer is simple: because flowers create lasting memories and make people—both givers and receivers—feel loved. Flowers also remind us that life sometimes goes by too fast and that we need to appreciate the beauty that surrounds us while we can. They teach us to live for today, because we do not know what tomorrow may bring. With a gift of flowers we know that someone is thinking of us in this moment and took precious time to show us how much they care.

Flowers are always present from the beginning of life to the end of life and in the best and worst of times. Life is always changing, and the circles of life are really just moments of time. By observing other's lives, I have learned so much and have been inspired by their strength and faith.

I will never forget David. He is a man with divine true faith and love. David and Cathy were expecting their fourth child. They were really hoping for a girl since their first three children were boys. Finally the big day arrived and their beautiful, healthy, baby girl was born. David could hardly wait to come into the flower shop to hand me a pink candy cigar and show me pictures of his new pride and joy. David, of course, ordered a large, beautiful, pink bouquet of fresh flowers. He was rejoicing in the blessings with the gift of life and was very proud of his new little baby girl. I shared his enthusiasm and was so thankful.

The following week David came back in the flower shop and ordered another large beautiful pink bouquet of flowers. He wanted the flowers to be larger and more gorgeous than they were the last week. With great concern he asked me to keep Cathy, his wife, in my prayers. Alarmed, I asked if she was doing okay and he shared that the doctors diagnosed her with a rare form of brain cancer. My heart broke and my eyes filled with tears of concern as we wrapped our arms around each other.

David was truly concerned for his wife since it could be the end of her life. I asked if he was going to be okay. He paused a moment and then replied, "Debbie, how can I praise God last Thursday and complain and be mad at God on Tuesday? I have to just praise God in my best and worst times. Today is one of the worst days that I could ever experience; what could I do or say at a time like this? Last week we celebrated the birth of our precious little girl, and I bought her flowers. So this week I can't let her think the worst. I need to buy Cathy flowers now more than ever to tell her how much I love her and to encourage and comfort her more now than ever, because I don't know what else to say or do." We just stood in silence for a few moments as though we were in prayer. I was just taken back and in awe of David's attitude, faith, and love.

I was so struck with compassion for this young man and heartfelt concern for Cathy. I reassured David that he was truly doing and saying all the right things. The flowers were going to encourage her more now than ever. Knowing what I know about God's love, mercy, grace and miraculous healing, I knew that David's faith and his act of praising God were going to help Cathy.

I just couldn't imagine what they were both going through. I was so inspired by their strong faith in the best and worst times of their life. It is moments like these that will never be forgotten - they change lives. Cathy was in chemo treatments for six months and is now completely healed. What a blessing! I learned so much through witnessing David and Cathy's strong faith in God. It changed my life to realize what flowers meant to them and that the flowers were touching their lives.

Flowers spoke when there were no words. I believe it was David's strong faith, the power of prayer, praising God, and realizing that the hand of God was reaching and spiritually speaking to Cathy through the flowers that healed her.

In the Eyes of a Child

Children especially need flowers today more than ever. Unfortunately, there are so many children growing up in stressful homes with a depressing atmosphere. The innocent eyes of a child see the beauty and hear the whispers of the silent language of flowers. They feel the love in the atmosphere, smell the freshness of the kindness and support. Giving flowers to a child shares something influential with a child; it expresses love through the flowers' beauty, smell and greatness. It shows the fragility of the flowers' character and life. As the child wonders in awe of the incredibly beautiful beings of flowers, he understands at an early age how precious and unique they are.

An English teacher named Cindy bought flowers for every student in her classroom on the first and last day of school. Usually it was the very first time in their short lives to receive a flower. It was so rewarding for Cindy to see the children's expressions and feel their sense of appreciation toward her. She believed the flowers were worth every penny, and her students were worth the extra cost even out of her own pocket. The value of the flowers was priceless to her students' ego and morale, and there was a peaceful atmosphere in her classroom with rewarding results in the children's reading skills and in improved grades.

Flowers also have a way of helping parents say to their children (or aunts and uncles to their nieces and nephews) "I'm very proud of you, "You are awesome", "You are so special and dear to me", and "I love you more than words can say." When a child performs in a musical concert, drama or play, or an athletic sport, consider rewarding their performance with a flower. You could also give a flower to a child for getting good grades, reaching a goal, or for their birthday. With this gift, they truly feel the love and support. When a child feels special and loved, their self-esteem is boosted and their heart is encouraged to dream big dreams with hope. Giving them a flower promotes these feelings. What about special kids who might not have the same opportunities as other kids with sports, music, or even school due to a disability or disease, or have difficult family situations? A flower could mean the world to them. They may never have received one before. That simple gesture covers them with a sense of safety, love and hope, and knowing that they are truly special.

A child needs love to help them grow like flowers need sunshine. I have seen struggling children receive a flower that triggers a sense of pride and encourages them to run and dance like the little champions they are. It is amazing how flowers help encourage self-esteem in any child's heart. Several years ago, my daughter ran into the house with a handful of dandelions clutched in her tight little hands. She anxiously exclaimed, "Mommy, Mommy, look what I picked just for you." As a mom and a florist, the thought and the gift of love behind the dandelions, even though they were just weeds, truly touched my heart.

If you want to change the life of a child, give them a flower and watch their self esteem grow. By giving a flower to a child you have just planted a seed of love into that little child's heart, changing the life and destiny of the child. The display of kindness to a child ultimately causes them to grow with a desire to give flowers to someone else. Ultimately, the child feels loved and is encouraged to grow into a beautiful flower.

When you give flowers to a child, the love expressed with the flowers will never be forgotten by the child. Children are our next generation. They love bright colors, tie dyed clothing, jewels, lots of glitz and glamour, which is why the rainbow rose is so popular. Every petal is dyed a different color of the rainbow. When these roses are in my cooler kids of all ages love to see them. The rainbow roses are so full of color that it gives them a sense of hope and color in a depressed economy. Children are starving for hope, color and a brighter future.

Children today need flowers more than we realize, now more than ever before in history. In their silence, children are crying out for the hope of the rainbow that will follow when this storm finally passes by. Teachers, parents, leaders: we need to love our children and give them the encouragement, support, and strength that they need and want right now. A flower is a good place to start. Every child needs a flower.

Chapter 2
God's Wonders

God is the Creator of all living things, the Author of all books, the Writer of all songs, and the Designer of all wonders. Flowers are one of earth's great wonders and are a gift from above. He created them when He created the grass, trees, and plants for your food.

Flowers do not serve any practial purpose for the human race. Yet to the sensing individual, a flower brings beauty, color, texture and aroma to the world around them. Like snowflakes, no one flower is exactly the same as any other. Flowers are a reflection of His love, beauty and grace. They are a little piece of heaven here on earth. When we share flowers with one another we are sharing God's love, and we give flowers as a symbol of His love.

As a florist, I have had the privilege of working with God's precious gifts, which we call flowers. When I let God be the designer and I the brush, some of the most creative ideas and masterpieces are created. In the same manner, when I let go and let God take control of my life, many amazing events happen.

Let Go and Let God

When I let my inner thoughts guide me I'm amazed at how His phenomenal ways touch my heart and the hearts of those around me. One such example pertains to a dear friend and client, Carlene, who ordered a spray of flowers for her dad's memorial service to be held in Montana. She ordered it in silk so that it would travel easier. Carlene told me about her dad's life, personality and characteristics. Based upon what she shared with me, I used a bouquet of country wildflowers with a cowboy hat, lasso, wheat and sunflowers.

When Carlene took the spray inside for the services, the family decided to use it as the family piece and centered all other flowers and memorials around it. After the funeral, Carlene told me how many people at the service stopped to gaze at the arrangement and were mesmerized by how the beauty of the flowers portrayed the man to whom they had come to bid farewell. Although the funeral and the time of grief were very difficult, the arrangement was a source of comfort for the family. Carlene's mother even wanted to take the spray to her home to enjoy there.

Soon thereafter Carlene's mother had an idea: since it was silk, she decided she would make small bouquets for her and her children to keep in remembrance of their father's life. She disassembled the spray and separated each kind of flower into seven different piles of individual arrangements, one for each child, and one for herself. As she broke apart the arrangements into the smaller bouquets, she cried, because to her amazement the spray contained seven stems of each type of flower. Thus there were enough for her and all of her children to have the same number of flowers.

When I make arrangements, I do not count the flowers. I simply make them according to what I feel should be placed in the arrangement. In addition, I did not know how many brothers and sisters Carlene had in her family. We did not communicate those details, yet it was as though the hand of God whispered in my ear the number of flowers to put in His masterpiece. Then, with my brush, I painted a ray of colors for the family to enjoy.

Moments like these, which are unexplained and phenomenal, warm my heart and amaze me. As with anything, when your heart is in your work, you become the brush used by Him to paint His masterpieces. I don't take credit for the beauty of the arrangements I create; it is all God's magnificent beauty in the beautiful flowers.

Butterfly Kisses

Another example of how God works through my designs is when I create a piece based on a person's character traits, likes and dislikes. One story in particular comes to mind because of its significance. A dear friend, Tim, referred me to his sister, Karen, who had suddenly lost her husband due to a heart attack. Karen was overwhelmed with making funeral arrangements and taking care of his business and clients. She was so busy, so we did not meet prior to the funeral. I didn't get a chance to learn much about Karen's husband before I created his arrangement. Karen put her complete faith in me, even though we had never met or done prior business, to create a floral representation of the love she had lost.

However, Karen did share some of his favorite things, likes, and hobbies, which included his love for gardening. The funeral was taking place in the summer, so I chose to use a garden theme with a mix of summer flowers and colors as well as a couple of miniature clay pots.

As I created this floral commemoration, a thought came to my mind to put a butterfly in it. I usually don't put butterflies in a masculine arrangement but something whispered, "Use a butterfly." Butterflies are always found in gardens and it was the perfect finishing touch to a garden masterpiece. When I finished the casket spray, I delivered the flowers to the funeral home, where I met Karen and her family. When she saw the butterfly, she looked at me in awe and her eyes filled with tears. The butterfly meant more to her in the moments than I could ever have conceived. While I was at the funeral home, Tim asked me how I knew about the butterfly story. I had no idea what he was talking about. When Tim told me what the butterfly meant, he had to try to keep the tears from overwhelming him. He said that the day before, Karen and her family were trying to relax in the backyard, having ice tea after a long, difficult day of making funeral arrangements. As Karen talked about how much she was going to miss her husband, a butterfly flew into her presence, floated gently in the air, and gracefully paused by her as though it were giving her a *butterfly kiss*.

Tim grabbed my hand as if to say thank you. No one knew about the butterfly kiss experience other than the family who was there in the backyard the day before. That's why Karen and her family were in such amazement that I included a butterfly.

There are extraordinary, phenomenal moments that no one can explain, and the moments make a person wonder how or why events such as the butterfly story happen. At moments like these it is as though God Himself is in the room, and His great comfort is touching their hearts and surrounding the family with love. Tim and Karen's family was blessed with a great memory. Months after the service, Tim told me that every time Karen sees a butterfly it reminds her of her husband, and it comforts her when she thinks of life as a garden.

As was seen in the butterfly story, God can gently surround us with love, grace, and beauty in the midst of our situation. The next time you see a butterfly, try to stop and enjoy the moment. Watch the butterfly as it gracefully flutters and gently kisses the flowers in the garden. The butterfly kisses will fill your heart with peace and joy just as it did with Karen. If we learn to take time for the little things God will reveal Himself to us, and we will find great comfort knowing that He is always surrounding us in ways we usually don't notice.

Everything Happens in His Time

When we think about our lives we often imagine our life happening in our own time. I have a friend who planted tulip bulbs one fall with her six-year-old daughter, Caroline. Each day when she got home from kindergarten, Caroline ran outside to check for blooms. Her mom told her to be patient because tulips don't grow overnight and she wouldn't see any tulips until spring. Caroline pursed her lips and mumbled, "Why did we plant them then?"

Many of us may be like Caroline in that we expect instant results. But what we don't realize is that God doesn't work according to our schedule. As humans with God-given free will, we all struggle with the concept of His time versus our time. There is a season and a reason for His purpose and His plans for everything. We may want things to happen right now even though it may not be the best time.

Have you ever heard the phrase "We have to plant the seeds today for all the flowers of tomorrow?" When we plant seeds today, we have to be patient with the knowledge and understanding that there is a season and a reason for everything before we can enjoy the flowers in God's perfect timing.

As with the story of Caroline planting tulips, it is up to us to plant the seeds and then in God's perfect timing, He will water and make the seeds grow. In relationships we need to plant seeds today of love and kindness. By giving flowers to someone, we plant a seed for our relationships to grow and blossom into a beautiful garden. It is so important to plant the seeds today. If no seeds are planted, there will be no flowers in our garden to enjoy with our family and friends.

As a Christian, it is so important to plant the seeds and wisdom of Jesus. In God's time He will nourish the seed of the Holy Spirit to grow in our heart. God wants us to plant many seeds by sharing the gospel, even knowing they may not always take root in the rocky soil of someone's soul. God loves the gardener who plants lots of seeds.

When sharing the gospel and planting seeds of knowledge we never know which seeds will finally land in the fertile soil and take root in a rich soul. For example, a farmer will only reap a fruitful harvest in the fall according to the number of seeds he plants in the spring. The more seeds he plants, the greater the harvest.

As Christians, we need to plant as many seeds as possible in sharing the gospel so that God can reap a bountiful harvest of saved souls. Sometimes we may not see or reap the labors of our hard work, yet it is so important to plant the seeds. If no seeds were planted, there would be no flowers of saved souls to pick from the earthly garden. When Jesus returns, He wants to take a surplus as He harvests the souls to His kingdom in the eternal garden of heaven. God is the gardener, and Jesus is the true vine of life, as it states in John 15:1(NIV).

God's Timing with Hidden Messages

God knows every detail, has divine timing, and a bigger plan. I'd like to share with you another personal experience of God's perfect timing that shows how He sees everything, and orchestrates the details. As soon as we heard the news of our senior minister's loss of his mother, I wanted to send flowers from our family. However, I knew that the church was supported with a large congregation, so Pastor Jacob and his family would be overwhelmed with flowers, cards, and food. Thus, we decided to send an anonymous gift.

The flowers were designed with pink roses, lilies and an open replica of a Bible with an inspirational poem on one page and Psalm 23 on the other. Knowing the funeral procedures, times of deliveries, and arrival of church and mortuary staff, I was prepared to deliver the flowers before anyone arrived at the church. I was hoping to sneak in silently and leave like a church mouse so no one would know who left the flowers—except God. The card was signed anonymously and placed in a plain envelope so that it could not be traced back to the florist.

To my surprise, Pastor Jacob and Miss Leanne, his wife, were there when I walked in with the floral arrangement. Seeing Pastor Jacob's response as he marveled at the unique flowers designed for him, brought tears to my heart. I paused, and in the silence, I held the floral spray before him so that he would have a moment to let the Holy Spirit touch his soul. As Pastor Jacob read the messages of Psalm 23 and the other inspirational poem on the pages of the Bible, the Holy Spirit whispered into his heart and the tears started to roll down his cheeks.

Then Pastor Jacob asked who had sent the flowers.

Not saying a word, I handed Pastor Jacob the disclosure card and proceeded to carry the arrangement to the front of the church as the lights in the sanctuary were just turning on. I asked God in my mind, "Is this your plan? Now what am I supposed to do?" I tried to leave anonymously and quietly, while he was reading the card of love and encouragement with no signature or florist. God knew, saw, and orchestrated this moment for a reason. God must have wanted Pastor Jacob and me to experience the gift of flowers given unselfishly, and experience the feelings of being so loved.

Pastor Jacob stopped me and asked me again if I knew who sent the flowers. I thought to myself, "God made them," because the flowers are not mine anyway. He created them and orchestrated this precious moment. It is moments like this, which are unexplained and unplanned, when God's plans reveal hidden messages. Not knowing how to answer the question, I pondered the thought.

Pastor Jacob shared with me how much he loved the presentation of the Bible, with the Psalm and the poem surrounded by the pink flowers, honoring his mother. As tears ran down Pastor Jacob's cheeks, I saw how much the flowers touched his heart. He didn't know how to possibly thank the person who sent the flowers. Realizing the plan was not in my hands but God's, I finally opened up and shared that it was from my family and that I designed the flowers. Pastor Jacob looked at me, confused, and asked why I didn't sign my name. I told him that I knew how much he was loved and how many flowers and gifts he would receive and that I didn't want him to have to worry about a thank you.

Pastor Jacob turned around and started to sob. He was touched by the selfless act of kindness. He felt God's love touch his heart as though it were an act of Jesus. I did not know what to say or how to comfort the minister. You see, I did not have to say anything - the flowers said it all. As I hugged Pastor Jacob with caring arms, the arms were not my arms, they were God's graceful arms of mercy wrapping His love around Pastor Jacob. God orchestrated the whole moment.

Not a word was shared, yet love, comfort, support, strength and thank you were expressed in the silence. In that moment, the hand of God touched him. Pastor Jacob did not need to say thank you; his facial response and tears of joy did that, and I experienced the depth of the emotions with which the arrangement of flowers touched his heart. When you give without expecting anything in return, you will receive tenfold and more. I did not expect to receive anything, and his response was more than I ever dreamed.

God wanted me to see Pastor Jacob's response and, for some reason, wanted Pastor Jacob to feel and know that God's love is always near in any circumstance, even when we least expect it or in the midst of brokenness. I don't know what the flowers whispered to Pastor Jacob; only he knows the whisper of God and what the Holy Spirit told him in that moment. It was such an honor to be used in God's plans and to have a hand in his masterpiece, and it was a privilege to be able to experience something even more beautiful than just the beauty of the flowers.

It is a challenge to surrender our time to God even though we aren't in control. Trust God, allow Him to work through you and give Him the control. God is the great provider and comforter when we let go and let God be the controller. We have to trust in Him to take care of us and trust that there is a reason and a purpose for everything. God's direction brings about total union with Him.

When we obey His will, we live at peace and have joy. In the steps of the Lord there is prosperity, growth, and salvation. Stop resisting what God wants to do in your life. He has already worked out the tiny details and He is doing it for your own good. He has carefully planted seeds in each and every one of us that, over time, will either bloom or die.

What Seeds Are You Planting?

Coming from a farming background, I know there is a season for planting and a season for reaping the harvest. Both can't be done at the same time. We cannot reap the harvest if we haven't planted the seed. Where are you in the season or the garden of life? As a flower, what are you?

You can be the seed or you can start planting the seed of love by giving a flower to someone. You can water the seed and watch the flower of love grow. As time goes by, you will see in return a beautiful flower giving more love sent from heaven back to you, because as it dies it will give tenfold more seeds for a new generation to plant. What a beautiful picture of planting seeds of love and kindness with flowers.

What seeds are you letting grow in your heart? What kind of seeds are you planting in your thoughts? What kind of fruits will you bear from your plant? Who will enjoy the fruits of your labor? If life seems like hard work, remember that you need to be aware of the seeds planted in your soul or in your thoughts; only the seeds planted will grow. For example, if seeds of pumpkins are planted in your garden, that's what you'll grow. Nature will not allow onions to grow from a tulip bulb or potatoes from a mustard seed.

I encourage you to take the time to plant a flower and watch it grow. For example, plant a rose bush, and watch it as it starts to grow shoots and produce new leaves. See how the buds start to form and swell each day until a beautiful, perfect flower is ready to be unveiled. See how the buds burst open and notice the color being transformed into radiant petals of a perfect rose bud. The rose will unveil unique beauty and a sweet perfume of fragrance will start to permeate the surroundings. Life is like a flower. Our earthly lives compared to heaven's time are relatively short like a flower's bloom.

Have you ever enjoyed a drive in a beautiful mountain area or grassy meadows? Do you notice all the wildflowers blooming in a variety of blues, yellows, lavenders or whites mixed in with the wild grasses, sages and evergreens?

My husband, Kevin, and I always enjoy admiring nature and all of its beauty. This was especially true one day on a drive through the mountains. During the early spring, after the rains, the landscape was a deeper green than usual. We noticed bright golden yellow flowers covering some of the meadows mixed with a variety of colorful flowers against a background of different shades of greens. They were breathtaking. In awe of the gorgeous contrasts, we stopped to stretch our legs. Out of curiosity, we decided to walk out into the meadow to see what the beautiful flowers were. When we got closer, to our surprise, the golden yellow flowers were dandelions! Beautiful yellow dandelions! As we laughed at ourselves, we realized that what seemed from a distance to be beautiful flowers were merely weeds.

What a perfect illustration of the perspective of a flower! Sometimes when we are close, we cannot see the bigger picture because we are too close. When we admire the beauty from a distance, we can see a beautifully painted landscape. This perspective is true in so many ways. Do we just see the flower blossoms, or do we see deeper into their souls?

In God's eyes, as He created them, the flowers and weeds are all beautiful. Sometimes we are too close and can't see the real beauty that we might see from a distance. From one perspective, it was just an obnoxious lawn weed; from another perspective, it was a golden wildflower in the gorgeous landscape.

What do you see when you see flowers? What is your perspective? Farmers and ranchers see a lot of weeds, while other people may enjoy the beauty of those same flowers—such as sunflowers or thistles—growing in their fields. Sunflowers are very commonly known as happy flowers. Yet a farmer works long hard days trying to destroy the obnoxious weed from choking out his crops. The farmer does not see joy or happiness in a sunflower.

The next time you see flowers, stop and notice your reaction to them. Do you receive an inspirational or emotional inner feeling? Do you see the close weed or do you see something really beautiful from a distance? "Stop and smell the flowers" is a beautiful inspirational phrase. Life is more valuable when it is seen from the right perspective. Sometimes being too close or living in the moment prevents us from seeing the beauty in the distance. Often times, our focus is on the "now"; the flowers are only here today and gone tomorrow. When you give a flower, you brighten someone's day instantly; in the distance, however, your gift lasts much longer in the heart and will never be forgotten.

Wouldn't we want our own lives to be reflections of a flower? When we are up close to a flower, we can see the true colors and brightness, and they notice the variety of shapes, sizes and characteristics. We enjoy the flower's fresh aroma but also see the real beauty of the love, joy, kindness, thoughtfulness, emotion and feelings at a distance. The heartfelt love given with that flower will never fade nor be forgotten.

Plant seeds today for all of the flowers of tomorrow. Right now it might be just a seed, but it will grow to be a flower tomorrow. When you plant a seed of love today, can you see the beauty in the future of the beautiful flower of love blooming? As flowers die, they always seed themselves so that new flowers can start a new cycle. Which came first—the seed or the flower? Where are you in the cycle or season of a flower? Are you the seed? Are you the gardener planting the seed? Where will the flower come from if no one plants a seed?

Open the Rose

A young person walked through a garden with an older preacher at his side. Feeling insecure about the direction God had for him, he asked the preacher what to do. The preacher walked up to a rosebush, picked a rosebud, and handed the rose to the young teenager and told him to try to open the rose without tearing off any petals.

The young teenager then looked at the preacher, questioning his intentions and wondering what the purpose was in opening a rose. Could it possibly have to do with his wanting to know the *will of God* for his life? Out of respect for the preacher, the teen proceeded to *try* to unfold the rose petals from the rose while keeping every petal intact. It wasn't long before he realized that it was impossible to unfold the petals of a rose.

Noticing the teenager's inability to unfold the petals of the rose while keeping the petals intact, the preacher started to explain the hidden secrets of life that only God can reveal. The preacher told the teen that the rose is only a tiny rosebud, a flower of God's design, yet he can't unfold the petals with his hands.

The same is true for us. We can't open the rosebud without tearing the petals and killing the flower. This story illustrates that if we cannot unfold the rose petals from the rosebud of God's design, then how can we think we have the wisdom to unfold our lives. Only God opens the rose so sweetly in His time and gracefully by His design.

We need to trust in God for His direction each moment of every day. Look to Him in prayer for His guidance to the path of life in every moment of every day. The pathway which sits in front of you and me, but only our heavenly Father knows it. I trust God to unfold the moments in my life, just as God gracefully opens the petals of the beautiful rose. God is the only One who can reveal the purpose and plans for the beauty of our life to gracefully open like the petals of a rose.

Like the petals of a rose, there are many hidden secrets that only the Creator knows. Even His simplest designs are complex - much too complex for us to recreate or even understand, though we may try. Did you know that people have tried to put all the kernels of corn back on the cob after shelling them off? No man or scientist can put the corn back on the ear and make it fit. Scientists have numbered every kernel, placed them directly in the same place, and experimented many times with different theories, yet they cannot explain the simple phenomenon of its creation.

There are so many other phenomenal creations that only God knows and takes care of. There is a reason why there are hidden secrets in all creation. However, it is impossible for man to understand because man is not the creator. The Bible reveals hidden messages and words of wisdom to every believer. The messages can be hidden from the wisest scholars, yet God reveals himself in the word of God to a child of God.

As written in Matthew 13:34–35 (NIV), Jesus always used stories and illustrations when speaking to crowds. In fact, he never spoke to anyone without using such parables. The Bible is full of hidden secrets, written between the lines, and underneath every parable is great wisdom and knowledge. So many times Jesus spoke from nature's perspective of planting seeds and reaping harvests. He spoke of good soils, weeds with the wheat, seasons of nature, olive plants, and all of the signs and wonders that are all around us if we just stop and recognize the meaning and the value of them. Jesus used nature and stories, so it would hopefully be easier for humans to understand the spiritual message from the simple stories of our physical surroundings to translate to the spiritual message.

Miracles

Miracles happen when you believe that with God all things are possible. God performs wonders that cannot be fathomed, miracles that cannot be counted. (Job 5:9)(NIV) What exactly is a miracle? They are unexpected but welcome happenings that can't be explained. Miracles range from simple to extraordinary moments; for example, a simple miracle might be being able to pay the bills for the month. An extraordinary miracle might be an unexplained healing from an illness.

Miracles manifest themselves in the midst of dire circumstances or simply surround us in our everyday lives. God is with us daily, He will never leave or forsake us. We are surrounded daily with miracles all around us in the seen and unseen presence in nature—both physically and spiritually. Miracles happen in the presence of God or when the presence of God is with you.

Yes, miracles really do happen. Expect them in your life. With true faith and belief, miracles will pursue you. You are the God who performs miracles; you display your mighty power among the peoples. (Psalms 77:14)(NIV). Our purpose is to walk in faith with a heart full of joy and thanksgiving for all His wondrous works. It was amazing to witness this book as a miracle growing and multiplying, and with my faith grew. This can only be explained by God.

Jesus likes to draw our attention to nature because He sees power at work. Humans have lost touch with or overlooked the simple and miraculous wonders all around us that are in the creative power of the universe. So many times we can take God and the miracles that He gives us for granted. When we take the time to slow down from our fast-paced life we will begin to see the miracles.

Flowers truly are a gift from God. He created flowers when He planted the seeds here on earth. Every flower has its own beauty of color, texture, aroma and characteristic of life. Not one flower is exactly the same as any other. Flowers are a reflection of His love, beauty, and grace to you and me and for people to use in sharing with one another. Flowers are a little piece of heaven here on earth. When we share flowers with one another, we are truly sharing the gift of God and His love for us through the beauty of a flower.

Chapter 3
Bloom Wherever You Are Planted

Have you ever noticed the wildflowers alongside the road while driving down the highway during the spring? It's as though God took a paintbrush and dotted the roadside with yellow, purple, blue and pink colors. While paying attention to even the slightest of details, He delicately paints a beautiful landscape. One of the reasons I love wildflowers so much is because they bloom where they are planted. Wildflowers are not planted in a special garden where someone waters, feeds, and tends to them; instead, they grow in the most difficult or extraordinary circumstances where so many are not even seen, like between rocks, on the side of a cliff, or behind the most barren landscape. Wildflowers are not planted by the hands of man but rather by the hands of God.

God has a plan and purpose for every single flower He plants. Flowers provide beauty in the landscapes around us. Flowers bloom wherever they are planted in different soils, different circumstances and in a variety of conditions. Just as God has a purpose for every flower to bloom where it is planted, we are supposed to bloom wherever we are planted.

God knows the circumstances and the conditions of our lives and the places we are planted. God is willing to help us with any situation or environment. It does not matter how trivial we think certain events or circumstances may be. In the Bible, the Holy Spirit is called "the Helper." It is the Holy Spirit's job to help us determine our purpose in life and give us strength to bloom in spite of whatever conditions are around us.

Maybe you have been feeling like you are living in a colorless world in a barren land. You need to put your faith in God before you start to see color and a beautiful world. Life is so much more radiant when you begin to trust in God's purpose and plans. God has extraordinary plans for each and every one of us. Jesus said, "With man this is impossible, but with God all things are possible." (Matt.19:26) (NIV) If you know that anything is possible, your eyes will start to see life from a whole new perspective. You will become what God wants you to be with great purpose for your life. If you truly want to be guided by God you must first put your faith in the Lord. Let Him guide you into the job or the place where He wants you to bloom.

Jesus enjoyed the gardens and the beauty of nature surrounding Him. Jesus' use of nature in parables was one of His tools to explain and expand people's understanding of where and how God resided in the world. Jesus encouraged those willing to hear to let go of their anxiety and find comfort and encouragement in the knowledge of God's power, plans and purposes.

In Luke 12:27 (KJV), Jesus was speaking, "Consider walking into the lilies of the field, look at the wildflowers in how they grow; they neither toil nor spin, they do not fuss with their appearance, look how beautiful they are clothed— have you ever seen color and design quite like it? If God gives so much attention to the wildflowers, most of them never even seen, don't you think He cares as much for you, takes pride in you, will do His best for you? Yet I tell you not even Solomon, in all his glory, was dressed like one of these."

It is so comforting and encouraging to share this message from Jesus. If God cares so much for the wildflowers, then it cannot even be measured how much God truly loves you and me. It is beautiful to look at the wildflowers growing between rocks, in the crack of pavements or sidewalks, and on the side of mountains. Not only are flowers beautiful, flowers grow in perfect harmony with the world around them.

The flowers display such beauty to our eyes, while our lives display such beauty to God's eyes. When was the last time you took the time to marvel at the beauty of the wildflowers growing around you? Take the time to enjoy the beauty of any flowers so delicately planted.

As for me, I have the privilege of working with some of His wonders, which we call flowers. I take great pride, honor and compassion with every flower arrangement that I design. For example, if I'm designing a memorial arrangement, I place myself in the situation, with my heart and feelings in the floral design as though it were my husband, wife, mom, dad, brother, sister, son, daughter, friend or family.

I think it is a great honor and privilege to have the responsibility to prepare flowers in memory of someone's life. Flowers are a beautiful reflection of a loved one's life, combined with all the loving memories of life's moments shared together. The family or friends want the best display possible in memory of their loved one's life. It is a privileged responsibility to be the hands involved in designing the commemorative memorial arrangement.

Flowers express the right meaning without saying a word. I have experienced several extraordinary instances in which flowers have whispered a silent language to the brokenhearted. Occasionally, I will have an instinct and I have learned to respond to my inner intuition. When I do, I am amazed at the results. There is a purpose and a reason for everything. It's not just a coincidence when my intuition nudges me. God has a definite plan for your life and for mine. He will be the One to guide every step of the way into the fulfillment of that plan!

Budding Blossom

One of the first questions we ask ourselves as we begin to awaken to our potential is why we are here. What is God's purpose for us? This is a beautiful and wonderful question to ask. At some point in life, we will have a longing in our heart to know the answer to God's purpose. We'll question, "How do I begin to walk in a new direction?" In these times, there usually is a feeling of God's love stirring in our heart from the Holy Spirit. When we first begin to feel the stirrings of God's love in our hearts, we think about how we can live our lives to glorify Him.

Suddenly, instead of being just a mother or father, a son or daughter, a wife, a child, or a brother or sister, we discover that we are so much more. We have been placed on this earth and created in His image with infinite possibility and infinite potential. I know that my purpose is to let as many people as possible know the silent, whispered language of flowers and the ways that flowers touch other people's hearts and lives through the gift of giving flowers.

As a child, I remember the magical feeling of being in the presence of flowers. Flowers always seemed to captivate my attention with admiration and wonder. I became interested in learning everything about every unique flower and being close to or doing activities with flowers became a passion of mine. When I realized the joy that filled my heart when I was near flowers I knew that my career would somehow be involved in the floral industry.

My purpose is to serve as a passionate heart care giver for people during the best of times and during the most difficult times in their lives. It is a privilege to let the community become our family.

After my family sold the flower shop, I felt lost in the world and unsure of the direction God wanted me to go. I realized there was a deeper meaning to my possessive passion to be near flowers. It was not the physical work of the business that I missed. It was instead the expression of what flowers do for me and for other people that I missed the *most*.

During a discussion with my pastor, Christie, about my mid-life crisis, she compared me to a nurse. As she explained the similarities of a nursing profession and my florist profession, I understood God's purpose for me. Christie explained to me that just because a nurse retires from her profession doesn't mean that they can no longer take care of people. She told me that my way of taking care of people was through flowers.

God has given everyone a gift or talent to be used as a blessing to serve others. Even though the floral business sold, I still had a warm passion to be near flowers and to be involved in the rewarding joy of giving flowers to people. When I'm creating a gift of love, I'm also achieving harmony, balance, and peace in my life and in the world around me. I know that my soul resonates with the souls of the people for whom I am arranging the flowers.

Some of my richest rewards as a florist are not only designing a floral arrangement with beautiful flowers but also making the deliveries! The greatest joy is experiencing people's reactions when they receive the gift of flowers. I love watching people's faces light up when I tell them "I have a flower delivery for *you*!" The expressions are priceless, from the joy of surprise to tears of gratitude. It is a beautiful moment experiencing the love being expressed through the gift of flowers.

When God's purpose for you starts to bloom in your heart, you will begin to express yourself in serving others with the gifts and talents that God has given you to use. You will find more joy in your heart through the act of giving than through receiving rewards or acknowledgments.

Following the Call

It is amazing to me to acknowledge the prophets whom God used throughout the Bible. The prophets God chose, such as Moses or Abraham, were ordinary people like you and me. Regardless of the previous mistakes the prophets had made along the way, God still used ordinary people for a greater purpose. For example, Moses didn't feel worthy of bringing the Israelites out of Egypt, but God gave him the words of strength, wisdom, courage, faith, direction and power to perform miracles in spite of all of his weaknesses. God calls ordinary people whether they feel qualifed for the call or not, and God will qualify the called.

In Matthew 6:33(NIV) it says, "But seek first his kingdom and his righteousness, and all these things will be given to you as well." Seek His Kingdom" refers to seeking Jesus (God) first, and His righteousness, and to all these things refers to the blessings and gifts that will be given to you. You and I can be like the disciples and choose to follow Jesus. God will bless us with everything we need through the Holy Spirit giving strength, wisdom, purpose, direction, protection, skills and talents, gifts of blessings and eternal life. When I have sought Jesus and His righteousness, I have been very blessed with gifts and talents—spiritually, physically, professionally, mentally, and with increasing faith, strength, direction, and courage, in spite of all my weaknesses or failures in the past (and the present).

In Matthew 7:7–8, (NKJV) "Ask, and it will be given to you; seek, and you will find; knock, and it will be opened to you. For everyone who asks receives, and he who seeks finds, and to him who knocks it will be opened." If you believe that God has a purpose for you, knock, and the door will be opened.

When you put God first in everything that you do, He will guide your steps. You will not use your own wisdom, knowledge, and understanding, but rather God's gifts and talents will be revealed to you. As you move into a more conscious alignment with God's purpose for your life, a greater light fills your body, mind, and consciousness.

Whether you are called to work for yourself or for a company, realize that God is your boss. This means that we all are called to work for God in everything we do. We should do our best, as though we are doing it for the Lord. For example, we should clean our homes as though it were His house, farm as though it were His ground, build a house as though it were for Him, sing songs as though they were for Him to hear, or work for the company as though He were the boss. What is God asking you to do to serve others? Trust in Him, and He'll give you what you need!

For every door closed, He opens another one. My husband, Kevin, and I have experienced closed doors. When we first began our journey with *Flowers Whisper* we encountered a large amount of financial difficulty. Everything that could have gone wrong, did. Our furnace broke and had to be replaced. Then we needed a second mortgage, and then the next day we had four feet of snow which kept us from harvesting the hay in our fields. Finally, when we could get to the hay, our tractor stopped working. We felt overwhelmed. But what came through these closed doors was a chance for me to focus on the message that I wanted to spread with my book. God has never failed to keep us afloat and open the door to the next step in our walk with Him when the time was right. God resurrected the life of *Flowers Whisper*, which was truly an amazing testimony of his mighty strength of love and grace. This will always be the case for you, too.

The Bible tells us that we can hand over all of our burdens and cares to the Lord, because He takes complete care of us from the moment we fully surrender everything over to Him. So our job is to now live each day to its fullest and do the best, and be the best, at whatever God is calling us to do. If you can keep this kind of mindset, you'll be less likely to feel down or scared when things don't go the way you think they should.

"The Lord will guide you continually ..." (Isa. 58:11) (NKJV). It is God's job to guide and direct your steps in this life. The harmony of fulfilling God's purpose brings peace, joy, gratitude, and blessing to all those whom you touch. God's great gift to us is that we may be blessed and bless others in return, spreading love and light to each other and to the entire world. All of this is given to you free of charge. This is why you can let go and let God take control.

When God calls us to work for Him, be glad and do it obediently. Since we are in the will of God, we have to prosper. Sometimes we get out of focus when God starts prospering us. Understand that whatever God does for you it is so that you can spread the word of God to the nations. As a result, many will come to know God and live victorious lives.

Many people would naturally assume that flowers and God's purpose aren't linked. But for me they are, because flowers give me an avenue for creating a better world. Perhaps you had an inkling that I waded into the shallow end of the theological pool talking about flowers as a spiritual experience. Maybe you are not aware that whenever God's Spirit is made tangible, there is beauty to behold if you are willing to see it.

Jesus was certainly not above enjoying the beauty surrounding Him or using beauty as a tool to expand people's understanding of where and how God resided in their world. He encouraged those willing to hear to let go of their anxiety and to, "Consider the lilies of the field, how they grow; they neither toil nor spin, yet I tell you even Solomon in all his glory was not arrayed like one of these (Luke 12:27) (NKJV)." Each of the gospels points out how Jesus used beauty as a practical teaching tool and saw beauty in people's souls. It is poetic to look beyond what others see and feel the depth of truth that lies within living beings, whether they are flowers or animals or are women, children and men.

We are called to be the best and to give the most beautiful parts of ourselves to whatever purpose we are here to serve. Beauty is often pushed aside in favor of the harsh realities that overwhelm us, even on our best days. But God did not separate out the beautiful from the practical in the process of and He never told us to either. If either were true, nature would not provide such endless supplies of beautiful flowers.

There is a reason for my being. It is to express love for my neighbor, God and myself through flowers. When I express my spirit through the flowers with my gifts and talents, I touch other people's hearts with love. My gifts and talents blossomed when I realized the possessive passion I have for flowers as from God.

When I look at life through God's eyes, I operate my life from a different perspective and enjoy serving others. Once you start to acknowledge your talents and accept the gifts God has given you, you will start to blossom into God's spiritual purpose and plans. Once you allow yourself to receive His words, you will see, feel, and experience new revelations in your own understanding of who God is and who you are.

Blossoms Bloom

You are not just a number in a crowd. You are one of a kind. I do not believe anyone lives life between an alarm clock and a time clock. You will find your purpose when you take the time to look at what you can do for others. By serving someone else, you will be blessed spiritually and financially. Every business, person or job serves people in some way. You and I are here on the earth to serve other people. Jesus came to serve, not to be served. The first step to finding your purpose is to serve other people's needs. Wealth is not always defined by the amount of money you have but in having a life rich in meaningful relationships.

Many people live life without a purpose between alarm clocks and time clocks. You don't know how long you are going to live, and if you don't love what you are doing and don't find joy in serving, then how long is it going to take for you to make a change in your life? If you have a longing desire to serve the Lord, God will give you the desires in your heart. If you feel a strong connection to a particular job, follow your heart and immerse yourself in the longing and in following the path to the job. God will start revealing to you the answers to the questions you seek and will open the doors to opportunities. We are called to give the best, the most beautiful parts of ourselves to whatever purpose we are here to serve.

We dance together as God's people, giving and receiving from one another all the beautiful gifts and talents that we have been given. "Delight yourself also in the Lord, and He shall give you the desires of your heart. Commit your way to the Lord, trust also in Him, and He shall bring it to pass ... Rest in the Lord, and wait patiently for Him" (Ps. 37:4, 7) (NKJV).

God already has your next job ready and planned for you. You simply will have to seek, ask and knock before the door will be opened to receive His glory, and in His time, He will bring it to you. If you are searching for a job, look internally for God's wisdom and faith. Trust in Him and God will guide you to where He wants you to be planted. When doors close to job opportunities, interviews, or promotions, try to not be frustrated or discouraged, for God will always open the door to opportunities where He wants you to be. God will provide the nourishment you need to grow like a wildflower when you are truly where God wants you to be.

Our job is to live life to the fullest each day and to do the best and be the best at whatever God is calling us to do. By doing so, we will find harmony in fulfilling God's purpose, bringing blessings to all those we touch. This is one aspect of God's will, for us to spread love and light to each other and to the entire world. When we are called to work, we should rejoice and be obedient to the call. In serving others, we will then be blessed physically, spiritually, financially and eternally. When you put God first in everything that you do He will guide your steps. Maybe you are not aware that whenever God's Spirit is made tangible there is beauty to behold if you are willing to see it.

Many people would likely question flowers having a purpose or being used as an aspect of a greater plan. Flowers bring beauty wherever they are planted, therefore creating a better world and a more beautiful place. I encourage you to live your life like the wildflower, bloom wherever God has planted you today and brighten the world around you with your exquisite beauty that only you can share.

If you want to brighten the world and make it a better place, start by taking the first step. Is there someone you know right now, neighbor, family or friend, who needs your expression of love or support on anything? When we live in the truth, welcoming the vast creation of the surroundings in which we live, God will reveal the beauty in creation as we grow like a wildflower in the grace of perfect harmony, balance, and peace.

Chapter 4
To Give Is to Receive

If you truly want to feel love as a receiver you will have to first give love with the heart of a true giver. David Viscott once said, "To love and be loved is to feel the sun from both sides." It is a beautiful feeling to love and be loved at the same time. Giving flowers is one of the inspired ways to express love and be loved at the same time.

Have you ever heard of the term "givers gain"? Givers abundantly gain physical material items, spiritual blessings, emotional support, financial increases and reward with everlasting memories. One example of a giver's reward is the blessing of money for abundantly sharing their finances. Individuals who give flowers are some of the kindest, most loving human beings you will ever meet. Those people are also loved in return even more so. In all of my years in the floral industry, I have rarely experienced a grumpy or angry person ordering flowers. Never once have I delivered flowers because of hate, anger or ill will. Flowers are always given out of love, and they give love for any occasion. Being the florist is like being the intermediary, whatever the occasion may be, as love is being shared between the giver and the receiver.

Flowers reignite the flicker of love between relationships. When bridges need to be mended, words need to be forgotten, egos have gotten in the way, pride needs to be broken, or mistakes need to be forgiven, flowers are the perfect tool. I have seen flowers save marriages as well as relationships in professional business. When the argument has gone too far, bad words have been exchanged, or hearts have been broken, flowers help mend the situation.

Flowers are also a peace offering when a silent treaty needs to be signed. Flowers help build or mend bridges between neighbors, businesses, family, and friends. Just like the saying, "An apple a day keeps the doctor away," the same is true for flowers: "A flower a day keeps the attorneys and counselors away."

He Loves Me, He Loves Me Not

One petal, "he loves me," the next petal, "he loves me not," and so on to the final petal to know the result. Have you ever used this strategy when plucking the petals off a flower to determine whether or not that special someone loved you? Maybe you silently prayed that the last petal would be "he loves me."

Valentine's Day is the single most celebrated "love holiday" for everyone. I'm passionate to encourage people to buy flowers for Valentine's Day, knowing the secret of expressing love through the silent language of flowers. Valentine's Day is an opportunity to tell someone special how deeply you love them. Flowers whisper love and emotionally influence the one you love more than chocolates or balloons. One rose says "I love you" as well as a whole dozen does.

Flowers, however, aren't only for holidays. Love can be expressed in the impressionable dozen of roses or the extravagant bouquet every day. Remember, a single flower whispers, "I love you," any time of the year. Surprise someone you love by giving flowers without an occasion. Give a gift of love.

Money Well Spent

Is there any "other" gift on this planet as appropriate for just about any occasion as a flower? Think about it: even a gift of cold hard cash is not as versatile and appreciated as flowers are. For instance, you would never send money to a family grieving over the loss of a loved one, would you? Likewise, jewelry and chocolates would not be appropriate to send to comfort the grieving family.

Flowers are priceless because they repair relationships, strengthen marriages, express love to friends and family, increase business, heal the sick, touch the soul, comfort the brokenhearted and celebrate joy in the best of times. How can you put a value on flowers when they have such miraculous results?

Many children were educated about the value of flowers from an early age. When you were a child, how did your parents or grandparents value flowers? Did they enjoy gardening or growing flowers? Did they give flowers for different occasions? Were flowers present during holiday dinners or did they rarely buy flowers? Did they ever really enjoy the presence of flowers?

One of the greatest misinterpretations florists hear is that flowers are a waste of money. Some generations felt like it was not a wise decision to buy flowers during hard economic times. People of all ages would be reprimanded for buying flowers through remarks such as "buying flowers is like throwing your money out the window" or "why waste your money on flowers, when flowers don't last?"

Unfortunately, these statements don't consider the value of the love expressed through the gift of flowers. Money can't buy and express love. Yet flowers are always given in an expression of love, and they speak a silent language when no amount of money or words can express the depth of the love shared.

During poor economic times, flowers are not considered a necessity. Instead they are considered a luxury. I'm not suggesting that you should buy flowers before food or shelter, but it is important to remember and share the beauty God gave us through flowers.

There are creative ways to enjoy the presence of flowers without spending money to experience their beauty. One great way to enjoy flowers without spending any money is to visit your local florist or nursery and enjoy the fragrances of the fresh scents and all the beauty of the seasonal flowers. Also, you can take a relaxing drive and enjoy the flowers in your neighbor's yards or take a walk in a park.

Shane, for example, always takes his wife, Shelby, for a drive on her birthday in June through the neighborhood and parks in their area. Even though Shelby doesn't get any flowers for her birthday, she enjoys the fact that Shane takes the special time to be with her and enjoys the flowers blooming on her special day. To Shelby, her true gift is a relaxing drive through all of God's gifts. She jokes that her birthday drive is like driving around during Christmas in December looking at all of the pretty colors.

To Shane, Shelby is special like a flower. Just as God has given Shane the gift of Shelby, He has also planted flowers as a gift for us to enjoy for a day. It is a beautiful thought to acknowledge that the flowers in our yards can be inspiring and encouraging to our neighbors and to everyone throughout the summer days. There are creative ways one can enjoy flowers, making someone else feel very special without spending money out of pocket. I encourage you to take time to enjoy the beauty of the flowers planted in your own backyard, in the neighborhood or along the road during the drive to work.

God planted flowers for everyone to enjoy in the beauty of life. Take the time with your loved one, like Shane does with Shelby to admire and enjoy the flowers God has blooming on your special day. Shane shares a very creative way to give his wife the beauty of flowers without spending a fortune on a gift. The priceless gift of time, beauty, and the perfect reflection of love and romance is a perfect gift for any occasion.

Share the Beauty

Several years ago a customer of mine, Tom, brought in his own vase once a week to have it filled with whatever flowers were available or in season. He loved bringing flowers home to his wife and their family. Each week he placed his vase on the kitchen table for the family to admire.

Tom told me one time that there is something special when there are fresh flowers in his home. He can buy extra treats that he doesn't need, like coffee, or he can spend a little money on fresh flowers for the entire family to enjoy. He found beauty in the flowers, providing balance and harmony in his budget and home.

Have you ever noticed the number of flower arrangements at funerals? Some funerals have very few, if any, or some may have a beautiful display of many floral arrangements. The number of flowers present for a funeral does not reflect the value of someone's life or the family. It can be preordained by the loved ones left behind to ask "in lieu of flowers" or to request that no flowers to be sent for the memorial service.

If a family asks "in lieu of flowers," it is a recommendation to give money to designated memorials instead of purchasing flowers for the memorial service. The flowers are not for the deceased. They are instead there to help comfort and encourage the loved ones left behind who are suffering difficult circumstances. Some people, just prefer to give memorial money to memorials rather than to give or spend it on flowers for a funeral. Please don't misunderstand me, I think giving money to memorials is commendable, but I hear so many stories of comfort and encouragement from families who received flowers. Flowers whisper words of peace to the brokenhearted.

Long after the service, clients share with me the encouragement they received from the flowers being present during the memorial service. Flowers help and comfort loved ones during very emotional and difficult circumstances of death because they leave such a beautiful final memory. During the emotional stress of traumatic circumstances, commemorative money and gifts are forgotten while the image of the flowers lingers long after.

One client told me that she can remember the flower arrangements and the people who sent the flowers, but cannot remember the names of the people who donated money to the memorials or the amount of money that they donated. After her experience, she now sends flowers to her friends and family whenever they experience the loss of a loved one.

For those funerals that have many flower arrangements and sprays, I've seen families comforted beyond words. The brokenhearted loved ones left behind are comforted by the generous actions of people responding with love and support. Flowers tell the family how much the deceased was loved and will be missed. Flowers touch the family's hearts with the silent language of love and demonstrate a loving memory of a beautiful life.

Controlling Your Own Destiny

Can you imagine a wife getting angry with her husband for buying flowers for any occasion? There are actually some women who get angry or threaten their husbands for this reason. Usually, the woman has a lack of understanding, a controlling personality, or a perceived value of flowers as a worthless gift.

Understand that it is a natural instinct for a man to buy flowers for his wife as an expression of how much he appreciates her and loves her. If the woman feels strongly opposed to her husband buying flowers, she is in control of her own destiny, wrecking her own marital relationship and numerous other relationships.

Nick is a dear friend and a good client. Nick loves his wife, Janice, dearly. Janice lives with a strict budget, seems dissatisfied and unhappy the majority of the time, and is a chronic complainer. Nick ordered flowers for his wife several times on several different occasions. Nick had severe health concerns during the year, which required several surgeries. Janice was a great caregiver and supporter for Nick through several recoveries. On Mother's Day, Nick ordered flowers for Janice with a special reason and a larger message. Nick wanted to express the depth of his love and display his appreciation for Janice's unselfish acts of kindness throughout months of patient support through his numerous recoveries.

Unfortunately, Janice saw the the floral bill before Nick was able to pay it. Janice couldn't get past the price of the flowers and was angry with Nick and me. Janice could not see the larger picture from a distance or the depth of the beautiful message given by the most kind, giving and caring husband. Janice called me at the flower shop and complained about the cost. She thought the flowers were priced too high. During our conversation, I tried to explain the depth of her husband's message and love for her and the reasoning of the increased value of the keepsake container.

Janice was blinded by the price of the flowers and deaf to the words that Nick or I could express about the language of flowers. Janice ordered her husband to never buy flowers again. She let the price of the flowers dictate the destiny of her selfish attitude about flowers and ruin the atmosphere of their marital relationship. Her reaction explains the reasons for her depressed attitude with life. Janice sabotaged her own happiness by stopping the flow of the love being expressed in their relationship. One of man's greatest desires is to please his wife, mom, sister, or any other woman of significance.

As the florist, and friend, I tried to explain to her in great detail about Nick's desires and intentions. Janice was a very lucky lady to have a husband who genuinely loved her so dearly and ordered flowers with the intent of sending extraordinary messages. After a discount was given, Janice still harbored a bitter attitude over the cost of the flowers. She was deaf to the message and blind to the beauty of the greatest gift of love being displayed for her. Nick struggles to find the words to express his loving feelings toward his wife still to this day. Flowers can usually express the depth of love with inspirational messages except when the eyes of the beholder are blinded from seeing the real beauty of the gift.

So Simple

Men can also be blinded to the truth of the real beauty of giving the gift of flowers. Jason never bought flowers for his wife because he had a misunderstanding about flowers. Jason complained to my husband one day about never getting any sex. Kevin, my husband, asked him if he had ever given his wife flowers. Jason told him no because he thinks they are a waste of money. Kevin smiled and encouraged him to try it someday. After several encouraging words from Kevin, Jason finally acted on his advice and ordered flowers for his wife, Hallie. Jason admitted his frustrations about buying gifts for foolish reasons and wasting money on gifts that his wife didn't need. Well, to Jason's surprise, Hallie cried and shared how much the gift of flowers meant to her. Hallie was so surprised when the flowers were delivered that she asked the driver several times who had sent them. Hallie didn't know whether to cry or scream for joy.

Hallie was overwhelmed with emotions of being loved and appreciated by her husband. It was a complete surprise to her, knowing Jason's perspective and attitude about flowers. The flowers meant even more to Hallie knowing that he had bought them in spite of his bullheaded thinking and attitude about flowers. Jason realized that the value of the message being whispered to his wife was worth more than the cost of the flowers. Hallie needed to feel the appreciation of being valued for everything she did for Jason and their family.

Now Jason and Hallie have a much happier marriage because of flowers. Jason shared with Kevin that his personal success was also having more sex and doing more activities together. He told Kevin that if he had only known how simple it was he would have bought flowers sooner. The flowers spoke more to Hallie than Jason could have ever said with the kindest words. In fact, Jason did not say anything at all because the flowers whispered exactly what Hallie wanted and needed to hear.

Marriages that aren't blessed with the proper balance of love and sex seldom endure. Love alone will not bring happiness in marriage, and neither will sex alone. Jason experienced the secret and the missing link to their marital relationship, and now both he and his wife are more fulfilled. Proverbs says that finding a supportive wife is worth more than precious rubies or gems. Give her feelings of being appreciated, romanced, and loved. The country music singer, Kenny Rogers, wrote the perfect song, "Buy Her a Rose." It is great advice for men to take the time and just buy her a rose. It's the little things that will whisper that you love her. Sometimes a woman doesn't need fancy gifts as much as she needs to feel loved.

Flowers for the Soul

Flowers also whisper peace and comfort from heaven when the days are few. The end of a person's life can be one of the most difficult times to find encouraging words of comfort, so what do you say at a time like this? Sometimes saying nothing at all and giving flowers touches the person's departing heart to the depths of their soul. It whispers all the right words and takes away the worry of saying the wrong comments. Flowers comfort the departing soul more than you will ever know.

What do you get someone in difficult circumstances when there is not a lot of hope and the days are few? Flowers need to be present for the departing person to enjoy the inspiring expression of love and beauty. Flowers will gently touch the weakest fibers and remind the fallen of the love being left behind. Flowers prepare the way to heaven's gates as the soul is ready to go home. During difficult circumstances, it is hard to give the last perfect and impressionable gift. Patients do not need another knickknack, don't have the time or energy to read a book and don't need any balloons or chocolate. Most likely the patients want to feel loved and be surrounded by loved ones with loving tokens like flowers.

How do flowers whisper peace to the terrified soul? They calm the fear and anxieties of the unknown, comfort the loss of the broken and encourage faith and joy in the bliss. Flowers are little glimpses of heaven's enchanted garden.

We know that God loves flowers and being in gardens. In the beginning, life started in the Garden of Eden with Adam and Eve. Jesus loved to pray in the garden; Jesus was in the Garden of Gethsemane when the soldiers came to take him away. Jesus acknowledged being in His Father's presence in the garden when He prayed. There can be a spiritual encounter when one is in the presence of flowers or in the enchanted gardens.

If fresh flowers are nearby, individuals have shared the experiences of God's presence in the room, a sense of inner peace, a barricade of security and safety, an encompass of comfort, a palisade of joy and happiness, and a sense of strength, power and love. Words from the Holy Spirit are whispered in a silent language to receptive hearts. How do flowers whisper all the right words, without saying a word? Perhaps God, the creator, is whispering to the inner soul.

Giving flowers during difficult circumstances speaks a love language only the dying can hear. The inner spirit intensifies a deeper love that the departing will only experience when they receive the gift of flowers. How do you say goodbye during moments like these? Remember, the end of a person's life is a temporary moment in time in a temporary home. As Jesus reminded us, we are nothing more than a vapor in the wind.

Although flowers whisper to the departing, they also comfort the loved ones saying goodbye. They give the caregivers a sense of peace and comfort during very difficult circumstances. Flowers let a beautiful light shine through the darkness of breaking hearts. Caregivers have shared that having flowers present in the room during the final precious moments gives an unexplainable peace that surpasses all understanding.

Hospice nurses and staff have commented that having flowers nearby brightens their days with encouragement of beauty and grace while doing a very difficult job. Nurses try to comfort family but also need comfort and support during their difficult job. One nurse told me that flowers bring sunshine even through the rain.

Nurses, doctors and staff appreciate flowers more than they express in words. Flowers do more than whisper to the patients; flowers brighten the rooms by adding colors, bring sunshine into dark rooms, fill the air with fresh fragrant aromas and sweet smells of nature, encircle the atmosphere with love and display the beauty and grace of God's presence. Flowers remind the doctor and nurse of the importance and the seriousness of their jobs to do everything possible to help in the healing treatments for this loved one.

Delivering flowers in the hospital, nursing homes or any health care facility is one of my favorite activities. As I'm carrying flowers down the hallways, in the elevators and into the rooms, the flowers catch everyone's eyes, as though I'm carrying a little piece of the rainbow. Everyone notices the flowers and automatically assumes that you (the one holding the bouquet of flowers) are a kindhearted individual giving the flowers to a patient. Behind the smiles of the spectators watching as they secretly know how much the bouquet of flowers is going to brighten and encourage someone who is sick.

Walking around with flowers is like carrying a new baby or puppy. Flowers always attract people's attention like a magnet—note their eyes, responding comments, introductions to conversation and emotional smiles. Flowers bring feelings of love and an atmosphere of being loved.

Usually during the hospital visit with any patient, the conversation turns toward the beauty of the flowers. Patients are anxious to share the sender's name and the acknowledgments of their relationship with the sender. Nurses comment on the thoughtfulness and kindness of the sender, and they remind the patient to be thankful for the blessings of being so loved. Flowers gently humble the pride of the inner spirit to be a gracious receiver. The patient acknowledges the blessings of encouragement received and the deepest appreciation of the flowers sent.

As the flowers bring the warm sunshine into a bleak atmosphere, they can introduce a conversation on inspirational territory. Flowers break the coldest of conversations with the center of warm, loving thoughts and amazing beauty. It is astonishing to witness the attitude and the atmosphere rise to a positive healing energy when sharing the words of faith and encouragement instead of the negative circumstances or surroundings of the patient.

The staff in nursing homes and hospitals encourage the gift of flowers as one of the greatest medicines that family and friends can give for their loved ones. Usually, the loved ones are on a strict diet for health concerns, so staff does not recommend giving them food. Breakable knick-knacks are also discouraged because the rooms are small. The staff recommends giving flowers for the patients to encourage emotional support and a positive attitude.

Flowers are the best gift to share with a shut-in. Nurses, staff, doctors and family have told me countless times how much better the patient's attitude is with flowers. When people have a better attitude, it is a better day for everyone involved. Flowers instantly help patients physically, emotionally and mentally. Needa's dad, Felix, always told her that he would rather enjoy the flowers now while he's alive than when he's dead. Felix said he did not need flowers at his funeral, so Needa was ordered to buy flowers now for him to enjoy, and she did. Felix knew the secret to living life in the present and appreciated life to its fullest.

In 2 Timothy 1:7(NKJV) it says, "For God has not given us a spirit of fear, but of power, love, and self-discipline." During my journey as a breast cancer survivor, I was able to experience life from a different viewpoint, being on the receiving side of flowers. As a florist, I had always been on the giving end until my bout with breast cancer.

As life and perspectives change, the character and purpose is revealed on life's journey. It was more important for me then to have the humbling experience of receiving flowers, gifts, love, and support than to experience the giving experience. As I walked through my journey of numerous chemo treatments, radiation treatments, surgeries, tests, hospitals, doctor's offices and other procedures, a little glimpses of a greater purpose was revealed to me.

Knowing that God had a purpose for me to walk the very difficult breast cancer journey caused it to be one of the most valuable, blessed experiences in my life. Receiving the gifts of love, support, and flowers touched my heart and soul with an even more passionate desire to share the significance of giving love and the importance of giving flowers. I truly was able to feel the hand of God, see the face of Jesus, hear the voice of the silent flowers, feel the love and experience the support, comfort, and peace. The situation tested me and strengthened my faith with wisdom, knowing that God's strength and power is mightier than anyone.

While God was drawing me nearer to Him, He revealed a new vision to which I had previously been blind. Walking through the breast cancer journey changed my perspectives on living life. Life's greatest gifts are not in what is seen with the human eyes; the greatest gifts are in the unseen. For example, we cannot see love, peace, joy, or comfort. They have to be felt from within where the power of spirit must be felt through the heart.

Men Like Flowers

Flowers aren't just for women. Men like them too. Have you ever asked your husband, dad, brother, or friend if they ever received flowers? It will shock you; some will say, "Never, no one has ever sent me flowers," or "I don't know how I would respond if I ever did receive flowers." If the adult male did receive flowers, he would explain who sent the flowers, the location he was in and what occasion it was for as though it were yesterday. Some hard, toughened hearts have told me that flowers are just for women, not men. The idea that flowers are just for women is false and a great misunderstanding.

Men who have hardened hearts don't know the blessings of being loved, appreciated and respected. I have seen the hardest, toughest hearts broken and truly touched by the simple act of kindness with the gift of a flower given to an adult male. I have seen the tears melt the toughest man's heart as he expresses his inner emotions. Tears are not considered a reflection of a man's weakness. They are the windows reflecting his heart. The great misunderstanding that men don't need flowers or won't appreciate flowers is false because men have needs and emotions too. Men need flowers given with love to encourage healing, support, comfort and love just like women do.

For example, when a man has surgery or health concerns, flowers and plants are not what we normally think about buying them. Statistics show that giving flowers helps create a positive attitude, gives encouragement, shows love and support, and results in a quicker recovery.

Delivering flowers to men in the hospital is so fun for me. Their reactions are usually so priceless. They are surprised, generally speechless and typically emotionally touched by the gift of the flowers. Inevitably, they ask me if I'm in the right room. Men need the healing power from within as much as anyone else.

Typically, the most beautiful emotion comes next, as though the hand of God is touching their hearts. Normally they will respond emotionally, struggling to keep the tears from welling up in their eyes. A moment of silence and the toughest and hardest hearts are softened when touched with love. Flowers whisper a language of love, especially to men, with powerful words of strength and encouragement and the knowledge of being appreciated, missed and loved. Warmest thoughts and wishes are whispered to a man's soul through flowers. Flowers comfort him, encourage him and give him more patience being a patient. They help him have a better attitude, respect the nurses' and doctors' restrictions, discipline his behavior and recover more quickly.

Men are not fussy or complicated. Men like simple arrangements or something out of the ordinary such as tropical flowers or European-style displays. Men, for the most part, have a hobby or interest that they enjoy. The hobby may be something such as hunting, fishing, playing cards, golfing, sports, or racing. Flowers for a man can be as simple as a couple of flowers in a bottle of his favorite beer or drink. Men normally like chocolate or candy bars and also sports or auto magazines, which can be added to a colorful mixed bouquet of flowers. Be creative when sending men flowers. Adding personality and character to the flowers make it a better display, inspiring him with a heartfelt gift.

One particular delivery story stands out in my mind regarding men and flowers. Josh was having serious health concerns while waiting for a kidney transplant. He was in and out of the hospital normally for a month at a time. He was given a beta fish which he named Franklin with a flower at the top of the vase as a get-well gift. Josh truly enjoyed the living fish in his room and watched it swim around in the vase when he was awake. While Josh slept, Franklin rested in one place in the bottom of the vase, as though he was sleeping as well. When Josh was awake, Franklin would gracefully swim around, full of life, entertaining him and the visitors. Everyone visiting Josh also came to visit the fish.

Soon Franklin the fish was the center of every conversation. Franklin was entertaining for Josh and all of his visitors. The conversations were focused on Franklin, rather than on the serious circumstance that Josh's life was in. Josh did not know how he would have survived his long journey without the constant reminder of his family and friends' love and support.

Franklin was a constant reminder to Josh that he was not going through this alone. Josh was never alone; he always had Franklin by his side. Franklin provided a sense of comfort, constant encouragement, and a will to get through the difficult trials. Flowers or fish can help to refocus conversations from the difficult circumstances to a more positive topic.

Flowers give more than a gift that has no emotional value to the person you care about. A gift of flowers does more for the receiver than the perceived value of the flowers might indicate. Happiness will not come from the things you acquire throughout your life. Honestly, true joy and happiness come from receiving love and giving love to someone else. True happiness will come from what you give. A living is what you get, but a life is what you give!

Chapter 5
Stop and Smell the Flowers

"Stop and smell the flowers" is more than just a phrase. God gives us simple glimpses of beauty and moments of time that we should not take for granted. Life can sometimes be depressing, overwhelming and exhausting. God reveals Himself through nature, words unspoken, or a Bible story that changes your perspective.

The Bible is full of true stories that happened in the physical and spiritual world. Jesus always spoke in stories by pointing out the physical world around Him so people like you and I could understand and relate to His message. Now I want to share with you a spiritual story that influenced me and changed my perspective. The story didn't happen to me physically, but came to me in spirit. Before you read any further I encourage you to keep your heart pliable for God because He reveals himself in unseen ways.

My breast cancer experience was a struggle, emotionally, physically, mentally, and spiritually. Yet God revealed a spiritual story from within me. I struggled with the loss of both breasts and my hair and needed to take a break from life. In the story I decided to go to a park and take some time to get myself together. I sat down on a park bench and started to read a book.

A young boy stopped and stood in front of me. I was thinking that the little boy was about to ruin my quiet moment of self-pity. The young boy, all tired from play, with his head tilted down, said with excitement, "Look what I found!" Reluctantly looking over the book, I saw the young boy holding the most pitiful-looking plant in his hand. I couldn't tell if it was a weed or a flower, as the petals of the supposed flower were all worn and withered.

Acknowledging his treasured prize and wanting him to take this pitiful plant and go off to play, I faked a smile, and told him how nice it was. I then resumed my attention to the meaningless book. The young boy moved toward me and sat down beside me on the park bench, placing the flower up to his nose and declaring with surprise, "It sure smells pretty, and it is so beautiful, too!" He paused with a moment of silence, then said, "That's why I picked it. Here, I picked it just for you." The wimpy weed or flower looked like it was dying or half dead, there was not a lot of color left on the blossom, and the leaves were all torn on the wretched stem. I knew the appropriate response was to accept it and generously appreciate the token. I knew that I had to take it or he might not leave me alone or I would hurt his feelings. So I reached for the flower and told him that's just what I needed.

The young boy paused and smelled the withered flower one last time. Instead of him placing the flower in my hand, he stretched out his hand and held it midway out from his chest, without a reason or plan. It was then that I noticed for the very first time that the young boy holding his treasured prize could not see - he was blind. I felt my heart break, with tears pouring from my eyes as the sun shone brightly down on this young boy. I heard my voice quiver as I replied, "Thank you so much.

It was so very kind of you." I paused a moment and as my voice trembled, I continued, "You picked the very best one. It is just beautiful!"

The young boy eagerly asked, "Did you smell it? You need to smell it." I paused a moment, starting to take a deep breath to inhale the sweet smell of an old withered rose, and I exhaled, hoping he could hear my breath. The blind young boy sitting next to me was anxiously waiting for my response. I graciously replied, "It smells heavenly. It is the sweetest flower I have ever smelled."

The young boy smiled and replied, "I knew it was a beautiful flower because it smelled so sweet." As the blind boy scooted off the bench, reaching for his walking stick, he smiled and acknowledged, "You're welcome!" His warm smile was radiating a beautiful light into the darkness and filling his heart and mine with joy. The blind young boy could see the real beauty from the inside of the flower and was not affected by its outward appearance. Unaware of the irreplaceable impact that he'd had on my day and my life, he turned around and walked away, leaving footprints in my heart. I sat there speechless and wondered how that young blind boy had seen the darkness I was feeling and had managed to give the gift of a flower to someone like me. Perhaps in his heart he had been blessed with true sight. It was unexplainable—he had seen a self-pitying woman beneath an old willow tree overwhelmed in her own circumstances of self-indulged plight.

Through the eyes of a blind child, at last I could see that the problem was not with my circumstances or the world, the problem was within me. I asked forgiveness for all of the times I was blind and did not see the beauty with my own eyes and appreciate every second that I'm alive to enjoy the gift of life. I held the weepy wilted flower up to my nose and breathed the sweet smell of a beautiful, fragrant departing rose. I gazed into the inner beauty of the withered rose. I had previously been blinded by the appearance of the battered weed.

I smiled as I reflected on the memory of the blind young boy with the pitiful weed in his hand and realized I had a renewed vision to my spiritual soul, emotional feelings and physical eyesight. Like the rose, I felt pruned and battered in my physical womanly appearance, with no breasts and no hair on my head; now I realized that the beauty was not my outward appearance. The real beauty was within me. I had been blind in the darkness and now I could see true beauty in the light of the world and withen me. You see, I honestly believe this spiritual story is your story in some way, too. If you personally struggle with frustrations or disappointments in your own physical appearance or self esteem, please reflect this story, the eyes of a blind boy and the withered rose, as your story. The real beauty is from within you. God desires us to see true beauty in others and ourselves in the same way He perceives you and me. God's vision is seeking the beauty within ourselves and in our hearts. I'm so thankful that God revealed a message to me through the this story and eyes of a blind young boy. If life appears dim and dreary in any circumstance there is hope and grace - something beautiful is about to be revealed from within.

How many of us really take the time to appreciate the moments and gifts that life has to offer? Sadly, many of us have lost sight of the importance of the gifts God has given us. In a desperate drive to lead successful lives, make more money and buy more things, we forget to look at what we already have. The busier we are, the less we make time to enjoy and appreciate a painted sunset, an afternoon shower, a field of sunflowers, an ocean view, majestic mountains splendor or any other beautiful gifts created by God.

During a Bible study, our group discussed the sources of joy. Everyone shared the sources of their joy: one man mentioned his grandchildren, an individual suggested traveling, others mentioned a variety of sources such as shopping, reading, giving, helping others, enjoying their spouse or children, eating in restaurants, and other things. I realized that my source of joy was being in the presence of flowers and experiencing the joy of what flowers do for other people. I had an epiphany when I realized the sources of my joy.

We are often told to stop and smell the roses and to take a moment to recognize the beauty and wonders in life. But far too often we are so busy in life that we miss some of the most beautiful moments of joy and the blessings in our midst. If you become too busy to do and enjoy the little things in life then you have become too busy to enjoy and receive the largest and greatest things in life.

God reveals Himself through nature. We'll see glimpses of His handiwork displayed in the beauty of the landscape or the nature of living things. I'm fortunate; I live in Colorado and enjoy the spectacular view of the Rocky Mountains Front Range every day. Something magical happens when I stand in front of the breathtaking view from what seems to be the top of the world, or get a whiff of the cornucopia of fragrance from something as minimal as cut flowers.

Nature is proof that we are a part of something greater. God is the ultimate designer of all things beautiful. So how do you fully experience God's design? Stop for a moment and smell a flower. It is a lovely way to experience the depths and the splendor of God's creation.

The Last Rose of Summer

I have a dear friend who lost her brother several years ago on a crisp September day. Her brother was killed in a car accident when she was a sophomore in high school. In the usual fashion, an assortment of food, casseroles, rolls, pies and cakes flooded the home. Above all of the gestures of comfort, my friend will never forget the emotional comfort she received from a stranger. A woman handed her a letter wrapped around a single rose. She remembers that the emotions and the tears swelled deep inside as the words of the letter were imprinted in her heart: "I saw this lonely rose in my garden this morning. Beautiful, yet temporary, for it is the last of the roses to bloom this year. Just as this rose brought happiness to me this morning, I picked this rose as a reminder of your brother's short life. He brought beauty to all who knew him." My dear friend was deeply comforted and will never forget the words of the gift; the beautiful gift of the single lonely stem of a garden rose.

The rose is a beautiful flower recognized as the flower of love and beauty, yet it also has painful, harsh thorns on the strong woody stem. Life is like a rose. Some will experience the rose's beauty of successes, loving relationships, prosperity, moments of great joy and celebration, while others cannot go through life without the thorns of painful failures, broken relationships, financial hardships, sadness, tears, great loss and business failures. We would not grow into beautiful roses of beauty without the thorns in our lives to make us stronger and teach us to be better people. We need to recognize the thorns as blessings along the way and take the time to smell the roses during the challenges or difficult circumstances.

As I reflect back through my life, I recognize the failures and successes that have molded and made me who I am today. I would not be the person I am today without the thorns in my life. With every thorn or difficult time in my life, I learned very valuable life lessons that trained me to be wiser and more compassionate.

For example, if I had never experienced failures, I would not appreciate the successes. If I never had broken relationships, I would not love as compassionately or appreciate being loved. If I never suffered financial hardships, I would not learn the value of managing money wisely. If I never had cancer, I would not appreciate every day as a gift or be as compassionate for other women going through breast cancer. Without cancer, I would not have experienced the growth of love and support from my in-depth relationship with my family and friends, or my faith growing intimately with God.

Yes, I could've let the painful thorns and the failures give me a self-defeating attitude that destroyed my life, but I chose to not let the thorns crush my spirit or my attitude. As I was going through the difficult times, there was always something beautiful that life was teaching me. Life was not punishing me.

When I focused on the beauty rather than the storm, it was like wearing rose-colored glasses. Living life during the challenges or the difficult times can be some of the most memorable moments of greatness. Wearing rose-colored glasses can help me to focus on the beautiful, miraculous moments in the midst of life's storms and to appreciate the aroma of the flowers. I'm thankful for the roses and the thorns in my life. If I had never experienced the thorns, I never would've seen the roses along the way.

Do you realize that greatness is inside you? As Jim Rohn once said, "You must take personal responsibility, you cannot change the circumstances, the seasons, or the wind, but you can change yourself." Some people's primary problem is that they see themselves as a victim of life, where everything is inflicted upon them, with no hope for something better.

Faith has connected me with a level of inner knowing, which I had never experienced before in my life. With faith, I have learned through my experiences that problems are just temporary circumstances. We all have a tendency to try to change the aspects of life that we are unhappy about by changing the outside. To be truly happy, we have to change on the inside. I feel inspired and excited having discovered such a profound level of knowingness in myself and in my relationship with God. The only way to experience true faith is to investigate your own inner self and pursue a deep relationship with God.

Life is so much more! When we wake up and walk in faith, we live life to the fullest. Then we are truly abundant in all areas of our life. We are a part of God. Like a spark from a flame, we have amazing power within us to work for Him. You have unlimited potential and inherent greatness. You are a magnificent child of God. All you need to do is believe in yourself and follow your spiritual impulse.

Many people are unaware that the choices in our attitude or thoughts can either strengthen us or make us weaker. Our thoughts and attitudes can be seeds of greatness for success or self-defeating seeds of failure. A mentor of mine shared with me the story of spiders' cobwebs. With great wisdom, he said "The seeds of our attitudes and beliefs can be flimsy and transparent like the webs of a cobweb. As time goes on, the attitudes and beliefs can either grow like cables of strength or cables of shackle's that will weaken our spirit. Our attitudes and beliefs were planted when we were children by our education, the books we read, the movies we watched and the life events that we experienced. We need to plant seeds of success from successful people and learn from their experiences. We need to read autobiographies or study the lives of successful people who have experienced hardships, physical handicaps or disappointments. Wise people learn from other people's experiences. We can learn from their mistakes and we can learn from their successes.

Helen Keller, for instance, was blind and became deaf and mute shortly after birth. Despite her misfortune, she left a legacy of being an inspirational speaker and an incredible author; her entire life served as evidence that no one ever is defeated until defeat has been accepted as a reality.

Beethoven was deaf, Stevie Wonder is blind, Lance Armstrong had cancer, and but their names will last as long as time endures because they accomplished great success in spite of the obstacles they endured. Remember, many successful people have endured life with great hardships, physical handicaps or misfortunes, and yet they accomplished great success with positive attitudes and strong beliefs. The thorns in their lives made them stronger and more compassionate and were gifts to help them see and smell the beauty of the roses along the way.

The power of gratitude enables us to channel our innermost thoughts to overcome any obstacle in our way. We can unleash the power of attitude and positive thinking so that our lives are free of fear and anxiety. Our lives will become more satisfying and we will start to enjoy every moment of our existence.

All of us possess the power of choosing our attitudes and our thoughts and can respond with a positive reaction to our circumstances. If we focus on the negative areas of our life, we will be blinded to seeing the beauty of the good things in our lives.

Occasionally, the thorns on the rose stems stick us. There is a striking parallel between the care of roses and the care of ourselves. We have to spend time, energy and loving concern for ourselves so we can share our love with others. Misunderstandings, disappointments and discouragements can be like thorns on the roses; they can be detrimental to success and to having good relationships with others, if we let them.

Look at the positive aspect of your situation rather than the negative aspect. Once it becomes second nature to do this, you will begin to enjoy the magical moments in your life. You will become more content with your own being and purpose and will be more understanding of others and their individual circumstances and problems.

There are always positive and negative aspects to any circumstance in our lives. The choice is yours to either focus on the negative circumstance in your life or choose to appreciate the positive aspect of what you have and who you are. By changing your focus, you will find success, see beauty and experience miracles in your life.

Our spirits require regular pruning of self-centered attitudes or egos, which can be as hurtful spiritually as the thorns on roses are physically. The Bible reminds us of the absolute need of spiritual pruning. We are like the rose bushes that are unproductive and need to be pruned in order to produce spiritual flowers of greatness. There is a purpose to the thorns in our lives, they enable us to enjoy the beauty of the rose.

If we are tempted at times to give up on ourselves and others we need to take time to smell the roses and be reminded of the beautiful gifts in our lives.

Flowers remind us of God's beautiful gifts that are so abundant in our world. If we actively direct our mind to focus on all the gifts in our lives during the successes and failures, we will be able to smell and see the beautiful flowers blooming along the way.

Roses, Roses, Roses

There are over a thousand different varieties of roses. There are large ones, small ones, the climbing variety, the bush variety, yellow, red, pink, and on and on. Virtually all rose lovers will tell you the same thing: roses require time for pruning and lots of love and care, before they will display love and beauty and the sweet perfume of their fragrances.

The body and the life of Jesus Christ are like a rose. Jesus' body and life had to endure painful thorns of suffering and crucifixion on the cross in order for all of the believers to enjoy the beauty of God's love and grace in the resurrection of a beautiful rose (Jesus). Then one day we will enjoy eternal life with Him in heaven's garden.

There is great variety and diversity within this universal body of believers. I like to think that we are all roses planted by God in His garden. He cares for each one of us. If we allow ourselves to do so, we will blossom beautifully, each giving off a sweet-smelling scent, as the Son walks through the garden tending to our pruning and care. If only you and I could learn to "stop and smell the roses" like He does, instead of seeking to get ahead in life, the world would be a lovely garden just as He desires for us to have.

So, who among us smells the best to our God? Which rose should we favor the most? God has designed us to grow equally in His garden. We may grow in different ways, but we each offer a unique gift to the world. We are all different by design, but God perceives us all as roses in His garden. So bloom as He intend, and allow the other varieties planted in His garden to grow and do the same. Appreciate all of the roses in God's garden, no matter their color or size, and the world will be a beautifully colored place. Remember, roses might be called by different names and be grown in a different locations, yet they all have a purpose with a fragrance just as sweet.

The Meanings for Each Color of Rose

Red Rose

The most popular of all rose colors, red roses symbolize deep love, romance and passion. The red rose has long been a symbol of beauty and perfection and can also symbolize courage. A dark red or burgundy rose depicts a beauty that is uncontrived and unadorned. It can say I love you, job well done, or communicate sincere love, or respect.

White Rose

White roses represent purity and innocence, but can also symbolize reverence and humility. They are often used in bridal bouquets as a symbol of spiritual love, unity and new beginnings. White roses are also used in sympathy arrangements for funerals. They can convey something before heavenly, honor, silence, everlasting love, marriages and worthness.

Pink Rose

Pink roses convey a message of elegance, grace and gentleness. Deep pink often signifies appreciation and gratitude: thank you, gratitude, admiration and appreciation. Light pink signifies admiration, joy, grace, sweetness, harmony and warmth, sympathy, elegance, and gentleness.

Yellow Rose

Yellow roses symbolize friendship, happiness, joy, and warmth. Yellow roses can also convey a desire to start a new or give a relationship a second chance after a quarrel or misunderstanding.

Yellow roses also send a message of friendship and caring promise of new beginning, gladness, warmth, good luck, welcome back, remember me, dying love and jealousy.

Orange Rose

The bright and bold color of orange roses represents enthusiasm, energy and desire. Orange roses can also convey pride in an accomplishment or celebration of a new beginning or venture. Orange roses can mean fascination, passion and desire, enthusiasm and energy, pride, "or say I am so proud of you."

Purple Rose

Lavender or purple roses express the feeling of love at first sight. These unique and beautiful roses convey a sense of enchantment or something magical. Lavender roses resemble, regal majesty and splendor, wonder and impossibility, a soft spirit. Purple roses convey enchantment and magnetism, opulence and majesty, spiritual power.

Peach Rose

Peach roses can convey many different sentiments such as gratitude, appreciation, admiration or sympathy. They can also convey friendship and sociability. A pale peach rose can symbolize modesty, closing of a new deal, great cheer, sincerity and genuineness, sympathy, gratitude and thankfulness, and let's get together.

Coral Rose

Coral roses represent desire, passion and excitement. It also says "I admire your accomplishments" and represents good fortune.

Blue Rose

Blue Roses symbolize mystery or something desired but unattainable. Blue roses do not occur naturally and are artificially colored. They also represent ambiguity, the impossible or unattainable, "You are extraordinarily wonderful" and the mysterious beginnings of new things.

Black Rose

Black roses symbolize death or loss (there is no jet black rose, but a red rose dark enough to appear black). The black rose represents farewell and sorrow, loss and mortality, the death of old habits, the beginning of new things or a new journey, courage, and resistance, Halloween, and death.

First Anniversary, Lasting Memory.

I remember the first time my husband, Kevin, bought me flowers. I will never forget the moment or the gift. For our first anniversary, we decided to enjoy a romantic getaway to a local resort town in a hotel for the weekend. I was resting and enjoying the opportunity to take a nap in our hotel room, being newly pregnant with morning sickness all day long and working long hours. Meanwhile, Kevin walked down the street to a local florist.

Kevin returned with a vase of roses to our room and placed the flowers on the end table next to the bed. As my eyes opened to the beautiful image of the roses next to me, my first thought was that I was dreaming. When I realized that I was awake and the flowers were real, the surprise of the gift of flowers touched my heart and I started to cry. Kevin had bought three roses in a vase (a pink, yellow and red rose). I'll never forget the vase of flowers and the feeling of being so loved - it left an everlasting impression in my memory and touched my heart.

Kevin assumed that I would not want to receive flowers, thinking that the flowers would be a reminder of work. Then he realized that there was a silent language being spoken in the depths of love being expressed and he was surprised to witness my response to receiving the gift of flowers. As I share testimonies with Kevin of my clients' experiences with flowers, the stories have deeply enriched our personal lives and our marital relationship.

Flowers are priceless. How do you measure the value of flowers or love? Some of my favorite newlywed couples are the ones who start on their first anniversary and give a single rose for the first year, and then add a rose for every year after that. Unfortunately, the majority of the couples quit investing in the buying of roses after twelve years. Is the honeymoon over? No, the honeymoon should never be over. Couples should never take a marriage relationship for granted. The relationship is worth the investment for many happy years.

Love Grows with Every Rose

Lloyd and Becky are a perfect example of a couple that has been happily married many years. Lloyd only bought roses for his wife on their anniversary, and every year he added one rose. They have been married 53 years now. It is such a joy to see the love between these two special people when the roses are delivered. Lloyd decided the day he married Becky to make a commitment to buy a rose for every anniversary and add a rose to mark the years of marriage.

Lloyd remembers the challenges it sometimes was for him to have the roses delivered to Becky on their anniversary when he was serving in the military. He never forgot. As with many couples, some years were better than others, yet each rose represents the fact that we made it through the good and the bad, for better and for worse. The years are their memories that have tied them together in spite of whatever circumstances were going on. The rose represents every year. They recently celebrated their 50th anniversary with 50 roses.

To Lloyd, the cost of the flowers does not matter. For him, Becky and their marriage are worth it. Becky cries every time the roses are delivered, as though it were the first time the flowers were ever given to her. The couple sometimes travels for their anniversary and Becky takes the flowers on the vacation and enjoys the roses as long as she can. The marital relationship between Lloyd and Becky is truly a beautiful picture and words just can't express the depth of their love for each other as it has grown over the years. The roses are a priceless reflection of a perfect marital relationship.

Take note of the valuable blessings from investing in flowers—in love and in relationships, with the results inspiring a lasting relationship, growing with the one you love. One rose at a time.

One client always ordered 11 roses every time he ordered flowers. Finally one day I asked him why he always bought 11 roses and not 12. He told me that his wife is the rose that makes it a dozen. She knows that he will only buy 11 roses, not because he can't afford a dozen but because it reminds her of how much she means to him. She is the perfect rose in his life. I think 11 roses are a better gift than 12, especially after he explained his reasons. I want to learn to share successful ideas and to give encouraging secrets that help marriages and relationships last. I want to learn secrets and wisdom from the people who have been married 50 years.

Flowers are truly one of God's most precious gifts; they bless us with His glory and His presence while we are here on this earth. When we share flowers with one another we are not only sharing our love, we are sharing God's love. When we buy flowers to give, the flowers aren't ours to begin with; our creator has created them.

Cost of Love

How do you put a price on the life of a flower? It really can't be done. Flowers are priceless when you consider the value of love. There are numerous reasons why the price of flowers fluctuates over the year and throughout the different seasons.

Typically, the cost of various flowers varies with supply and demand. Ordinarily, there is a different expense in growing and harvesting each of various flowers. There is also a larger demand for some flowers than for others and some have a longer growing season, which will also affect price. The price of the flowers depends on a variety of factors such as length of time to maturity and the cost of pruning and maintenance. Expensive flowers such as roses have a larger expense in the plant care, take a longer time to mature, demand regular pruning and a lot of water, and need higher nutrients and fertilizers. The less expensive flowers can grow in abundance with less maintenance, less time to maturity and less demand which is reflected in a lower price. You get what you pay for because some flowers cost so much more than others. You are buying the life of a flower, and flowers can be priced by how rare or fragile they are, by the demand for them, by the cost to grow them or by the beauty of their blossom.

For example, orchids take a long time to grow and take a longer time to actually bloom their unique blossoms. Some orchids take years of growing to get one blossom while other flowers take little time to grow, mature, and blossom. They are also quite fragile as are flowers like gardenias and must be specially packed and shipped so this also affects price. The cost increases with the demand of flowers for seasonal holidays, especially during the winter months. The cost also increases when flowers are shipped from warmer growing areas or when they are grown in greenhouses or forced to bloom in seasons when flowers don't bloom.

Valentine's Day is a holiday during one of the most unfavorable growing seasons of the year, but the demand for flowers is high on that day. Flowers are forced to bloom in perfect harmony in unfavorable conditions or are shipped from warmer distant areas, which causes the cost of the flowers to increase. Mother Nature can also interfere with the growing, harvesting and the supply of flowers, which results in a fluctuation in cost. There is a reason for the cost of flowers as compared with love on Valentine's Day. There is justification in the cost of the flowers as it correlates to the value of the priceless love being expressed. One rose says "I love you," and a whole dozen says "I love you more."

When you send flowers, you send more than a beautiful bundle of blossoms. You send a message from your heart. The rose is a perfect choice for expressing the nuances of your deepest feelings. A rose adds a presence in a room with its scent, color and shape. A rose can take possession of the viewer's innermost thoughts and emotions, making everything else look absurdly small in comparison.

Do you ever really stop to smell the roses on the path of life, or do you just tell others to do it? I know there was a period of my life when I only gave lip service to the phrase. I can think of countless times when I brushed off an opportunity to let my children help me cook dinner, to watch a movie with the family, to take a walk with Kevin around the farm, to stop and read that book I had been meaning to get to or to enjoy conversations and relationships with family and friends. After my bout with cancer, I realized that I want to have the kind of life in which I stop to smell the roses and embrace the opportunity to take unexpected detours and savor those special, spontaneous moments with loved ones.

In order to stop and smell the roses, you have to see the roses first. If you're focused on problems and discomforts, you're probably going to walk right past a lot of little roses that God puts in your path. Several years ago, the entertainer Mac Davis had a song that reached the top of the charts. This song was called, "Stop and Smell the Roses," and it became his signature song. Several great truths are in this song. We need to slow down and realize that there is a whole lot more to life than work and worry.

The sweetest things in life are free and right before our eyes. We need to count our many blessings every day. As the song mentions, the road to heaven is going to be quite rocky if you don't take time to smell the roses. We need to spend time with our families and friends and let them know how much we love them. Life is really worth living when we stop and smell the roses along the way!

The next time you need encouragement or you are feeling the weight of the world on your shoulders, make a trip to you local florist or walk in a field of flowers and, with each petal, count your blessings.

Chapter 6
Find Your Sun

As the flower is to the sun, the sun is to the flower; as the soul is to the Son, the Son is to the soul. Where does your source of energy come from?

As we all know, the majority of flowers need energy from the sun to grow. But what happens when the flowers don't have enough sunlight to survive? Flowers have two choices—they either adapt or die. This is why so often we see flowers stretch themselves out in order to reach for the sun to soak up some rays of energy. Sunflowers are a great example of this, they turn and face the sun no matter which direction the sun is. One could say that sunflowers live their lives by choosing to live searching for the sun.

Unfortunately, many people are not aware of what our souls need from the Son of God, Jesus. Human beings lack the energy and power for the soul without the knowledge and wisdom acquired through the words of the Bible or by hearing the gospel. The acceptance of Jesus as Lord and Savior in one's heart is an individual's choice. The Bible reads John 14:6 (NIV)

Jesus said, "I am the way, the truth and the life. No one comes to the father except through me." We can either choose to live spiritually with Jesus forever or physically and spiritually die upon death. Jesus is our source of spiritual food and energy for our physical bodies and spiritual souls. You see, I believe Heaven is a real place and so is Hell. So which place do you want to go? It is your choice. God does not control your choices.

During difficult circumstances in our lives, our faith is also stretched like a flower reaching for the sun. As we grow, reaching and believing in the power of the Son of God, He will give us the strength and nutrients we need for our soul. This means that we will be working in the power of the Holy Spirit to share the Good News of God's Kingdom with the whole world like Jesus did. Prayers have more power and authority using the name of Jesus, which brings glory to the Father. Like the sunflower, we should live our lives by choosing to live with our souls by searching for the Son.

Son for the Soul

Perhaps you are uncertain about the claims of Jesus Christ. You may have asked yourself questions such as, "What is a Christian? What does 'born again' mean? How do I know I am 'saved'? What will happen to me if I do not 'receive Christ'? Is it true that all I have to do is 'believe'?"

You may believe what you have heard about Him and understand that He loves you and is near you. You may have even been raised in a Christian home and may be an active member of a church, but you may not remember receiving Him as your Savior and Lord.

Have you ever, as a definite event in your life, received Jesus as your Savior? Salvation is a free gift from God. Believe that Christ went to the cross - for you, taking your sin upon Himself and enduring God's judgment in your place. This means that God has forgiven your sins and you are justified in God's sight. Believe that Christ rose from the dead, conquering sin and death, and that He ascended to the Father in heaven to reign as Lord. Would you like to receive Jesus Christ as your Savior? Or, you may even want to be sure to have a relationship with Jesus. You may want to pray this prayer from your heart:

"Oh Lord, my heavenly Father, I know that I have sinned and have not obeyed Your word. I have tried to decide what is right and what is wrong. I have tried to run my own life, ignoring You and Your will for me, separating me from You. I am truly sorry, and now I want to turn away from my past sinful life and look toward You. Please forgive me and help me to avoid sinning again. I believe that Your Son, Jesus Christ, died for my sins and He was resurrected from the dead and is alive today, and He hears my prayer. For I know that I am lost unless You save me. I thank You for sending Your Son to save me and for raising Him from the dead. I invite Jesus to come into my heart to become my Savior and the Lord of my life, to rule and reign in my heart from this day forward. I receive Your free gift of eternal life in Christ. Please send Your Holy Spirit to help me to serve and obey You and to do Your will for the rest of my life. I pray all these things in Jesus' name, Amen."

You may continue in prayer telling God what you are thinking and feeling.

Trust and be reassured that having received Christ into your life you are sealed with God's Holy Spirit. You may or may not "feel" differently, but you don't need to. Your trust is not based on your feelings but on the authority of the word of God and His promises to you. Believe! This means that Jesus is alive today to help you live a new life and have eternal life with Him.

Living life facing the sunshine helps to encourage us to look ahead, feel the warmth of His love and not focus on the shadows either in the circumstances of our situations or our sins of past mistakes.

The greatest power is found in the choices we make. As the storms in life pass by, keep a positive attitude. May you choose to see beyond life's storms to uncover the sun hidden behind the clouds. If you choose to keep a positive attitude and search for the sun, you will find the source of energy to get you through the storm. What's more, in that moment you will see glimpses of the sun's rays creating the rainbow after you welcome the rain. Life is what you choose to make it.

The Presence

In my worst times, after a chemo treatment, my body ached so badly with severe pain in my bones and my joints. There were times when I could not find a comfortable position, and the pain medicine was not relieving the pain throughout my body. Hours after chemo, I was very sick with nausea throughout the next couple of days. At that point, I was not sure if I would survive the chemo or the cancer. Yet when flowers were in my presence, even in the midst of all the turmoil, pain, and suffering of the chemo storm, there was an incredible peace and beauty that surpassed all understanding. With the presence of the flowers, it was as though God's presence was surrounding me with His love and grace. Being aware of God's presence gave me the strength from within to persevere and endure the suffering. It gave me hope and a rope of faith to hold onto and the wisdom to know peace and that I would get through the storm.

With God present, I could focus on the beauty of the rainbow of when I would be finished with treatments. The flowers were whispering power words of love, faith, encouragement, hope, joy, peace, comfort, patience and understanding at times when I really needed them the most. It helped when I was alone in my hospital room, in my recliner in the middle of the night when everyone else was sleeping, or even during the long days when everybody was in school or working. The flowers were in my presence when no one else could be present. The flowers were whispering the most important language that only the blind can see and the deaf can hear. They whisper to the sick to heal, to the lonely that they are not alone, to the dying to live, to the heart to be touched, and to the faithless to believe.

Blessed beyond Measure

Even though my cancer experience was one of the most difficult times of my life, I can reveal to you the countless blessings I was able to experience. It was like an emotional rollercoaster most of the time; it was very challenging mentally and painful physically. Life was overwhelming during my cancer experience. Yet there was always beauty in the storm when I looked deeper or from a different perspective. I was only 38 years old, with a daughter, Krystle, who was 16 years old and a son, Warren, who was 12. I was in the prime of my life, enjoying the best teenage years with my children. With no history of breast cancer in my family, feeling healthy physically, eating balanced meals, and having no bad habits, I was taken by complete surprise with the breast cancer diagnosis.

After a double mastectomy surgery, doctors discovered that the cancer was already spreading. After I went through major tests, they found extensive lymph node involvement and a spot on my kidney, so the doctors decided to get very aggressive on treatments.

My oncologist was very concerned. He shared with me and my family that on a scale of 1–10, as far as risk for the cancer coming back, that even with all the aggressive treatments I was an 11. In spite of this, I did not let those words plant seeds into my soul. In my heart and in my mind I had too much to live for. I had so much more that I wanted to share and do with my family and the world; most of all, however, I wanted to do more for God and hoped that God still had bigger plans for me. The doctors proceeded to induce treatments with and the maximum dose of the chemo drugs that they could give me.

I put on my boxing gloves and told the doctors to give it all to me—the maximum dose, and the worst kind of chemo, whatever it took—because I have too much to live for! Knowing that I was literally in for the fight of my life, I had no other choice. What I was not prepared for was the beauty as I climbed that big mountain ahead of me.

Usually, I have a very positive attitude in life but this cancer blindsided me and crushed me into a cement wall. No matter what people said, I did not seem to hear their words of encouragement. Responding in denial, being stunned with my critical circumstances, it was difficult for me to comprehend positive thoughts. I can usually find something positive in anything, but in my shocked state of mind, I felt numb spiritually. While I was in my hospital room after surgery, someone brought me flowers. In that moment, I experienced the beauty of the storm, and the rain touched me.

In my circumstance, it was challenging for visitors to know the right words to say or the right flowers to buy. Yet in that moment and time, it did not matter where the flowers came from, the variety of flowers or who designed them. I love my job and I also love flowers, but I had never received the gift of flowers during difficult circumstances. When I received the flowers, the gift whispered to the depths of my soul. The flowers whispered the silent language with all the right words to me internally, emotionally, spiritually and mentally. I learned the principle of keeping my heart pliable for God: as this is critical in life. What I'm about to tell you makes all the difference in the world. God cannot be seen with spiritual eyes that are shut or blind. God cannot be heard, even through a whisper, by spiritual ears that are continually plugged or deaf to the word of the Bible or God with a hardened heart. The irrepressible God cannot touch the soul of someone, if the heart continues to be hardened by circumstance or disbelief.

Words just cannot express the overwhelming tears of emotional love that touched my heart. It was not until I was the one who needed to receive flowers and experience the gift of flowers that I truly understood what they mean. I have always seen the tears of joy and what flowers do for people, yet I had no idea what the flowers were really doing on the inside. In that moment, it was as though the hand of God just touched my heart. My eyes were finally opened to see the love, my ears were finally opened to hear the words of encouragement, my heart was deeply touched, my faith grew stronger, my attitude was emotionally uplifted, and my outlook became mentally positive, in spite of the fact that my physical body was experiencing enormous amounts of the pain.

The flowers appeared more beautiful than ever before. They glistened even brighter in my room. Believe it or not, one gets accustomed to the smell of flowers when working in an occupation with flowers. As florists, we get immune to the glorious smells with a few exceptions of real fragrant flowers. As I lay in the hospital bed, not nearly as close to the flowers as in my daily work, the floral fragrance was an even sweeter smell than I had ever before experienced. I could smell the individual roses, the lilies, even the carnations and the mums, as though I were standing in a field of flowers. The perfume of the flowers concealed the hospital aromas and filled the room with a heavenly scent. Perhaps the smell of the flowers was amplified so that I would not miss the message. God was whispering to me, spiritually, through the flowers. It is difficult to explain in words or express the magnitude of my experience with the flowers.

Friends and family struggled with the right words with which to encourage me during that time. Conversations seemed uncomfortable, sometimes unbearable, awkward and strenuous for the visitors to communicate comfort. Friends and family shared concern with extended family members so that they would keep their distance, avoiding the difficult situations and conversations. Perhaps only flowers can whisper in the silence. Flowers were constantly in my presence, sharing companionship with me, encouraging me, and brightening my day. They blessed me beyond measure.

Flower Power

There is power in giving flowers to the sick. Several studies have concluded that giving someone flowers improves the patient's mood and improves his attitude, not just at the moment of delivery, but long afterwards. Some even attribute flowers to the alleviation of some symptoms of clinical depression.

One study conducted three separate experiments to help determine the power of flowers. In the first experiment, 147 women were recruited (using ads in supermarkets) to participate in a study about "normal daily moods." In exchange, they would be required to complete a survey about their overall satisfaction with life and when given a gift. None of the women was told what type of gift they would receive. About ten days after they answered the questions on the survey, they received a gift.

One third of the women received flowers, one third got a fruit basket and one third got a candle. All of these gifts were equal in monetary value and aesthetic appeal. Upon delivery, one person handed over the gift while another person recorded the reactions of the women as they received it. One hundred percent of those women who received flowers smiled, 90 percent of those who received fruit smiled and 77 percent of the women who received candles smiled.

Three days later, the women were interviewed on the telephone again, and those who received flowers scored significantly higher on the mood questionnaire than did the other women who received the fruit baskets or the candles. The women who received flowers also scored significantly higher on the mood questionnaire and overall satisfaction with life than they had in the first interview.

In another experiment, a person stood in an elevator and handed flowers, a pen or nothing to anyone who entered the elevator, and then attempted to initiate a conversation with the individuals before they exited the elevator. Of the 60 men and 62 women who walked into the elevator, the men and women who received flowers scored significantly higher in social behavior and responded in a pleasant conversation as compared to the men and women who received pens or no gift at all. Those people scored significantly lower in social behavior and responded with minimal conversation. Another interesting aspect of this study was that some of the lowest scores recorded were when flowers were seen but not given—so it's not enough just to see flowers; it's the act of being given flowers that appears to affect mood and social behavior.

There are high and low spots in all of our lives, yet the most influential words are the words of encouragement. Flowers can slightly speak the best encouraging words words to us. Flowers can be words of encouragement to physical or emotional pain. Studies have been done in rehabilitation centers and sports centers. For example, the patients with encouraging people constantly around them increase their strength sooner and recover sooner. It's the same with any sports. People who have an audience tend to excel in their performance, completion, or competition. Bodybuilders lift weight in spite of the physical pain their muscles are enduring. They lift more weight when there is an audience or someone standing nearby encouraging than when no one is watching.

Studies have shown that athletes achieve greater goals, break morerecords, perform to a higher standard, and compete with a greater ability and desire to win when they have a cheering audience and the encouragement to do better. Anybody performs better and endures pain longer when there is someone nearby encouraging him or her. This is no surprise to anyone who has ever performed or competed in anything; it makes such a difference when you have someone encouraging you.

The same is true for anyone who has ever been through rehabilitation. The patient will endure, persevere, be motivated and push through the painful therapy treatments when constantly encouraged with the words, "*You can do it!*" Flowers speak a silent language of constant encouraging words to patients during some of the hardest physical and emotional challenges. Flowers can be the silent cheering audience, encouraging the depths of soul, especially when it is hard for someone to be nearby physically.

In a another experiment, a certain percentage of women in retirement homes and assisted living communities were given bouquets of flowers over a two-week period. The women were interviewed at the beginning and end of the study to assess their mood. Again, women who received flowers had a much better mood. Among the best medicines for healing the body, mind, spirit and emotions is a flower. This should come as no surprise, because nature is where we come from. Nature is literally the stuff of which our bodies are made, so it is the perfect tonic for our rejuvenation. For thousands of years the Native Americans lived close to the earth, honoring and respecting the way of living in balance that nature taught them.

Doctors and researchers have all found that amazing results happen and great healing occurs when people have positive attitudes and encouragement. So what can you do to have a better attitude? Surround yourself with positive people, think positive thoughts, live and work in a positive atmosphere or surroundings. Read positive encouraging words, take positive action, eat right, exercise, use positive energy to be a blessing, buy or give flowers to someone or be blessed with flowers as the receiver. Flowers are always the positive in any negative circumstance. The flowers are the blessings from the rain, the beauty of the rainbow, the good in the bad, the positive in a negative, and flowers are an up when people are down, and a light in the darkness. There is absolutely nothing negative about the flower.

The Sun's Rays Warming the Hearts

Flowers whisper the most encouraging words during some of the worst times. It is amazing to see how flowers say the kindest words when sometimes it is difficult to find the right words. In addition to the studies previously discussed, various other research studies have been done by hospitals and colleges showing patients with a positive attitude, or who have a great support team, who feel loved can get through some of the worst emotional or physical times.

For example, if you compare the attitudes of patients in the hospital who received flowers with the attitudes of those who didn't, you'll see a big difference. One is positive and upbeat, while the other is sad and depressed. When people have a positive attitude, they are better patients—nurses can tell you this. When someone feels loved, the results are amazing. The patients' recovery time is significantly shorter and smoother when they feel loved; it makes a big difference in the patients' physical healing.

Shelia, a cancer survivor, talked about all the emotional and physical swings of chemo treatments, surgery, etc. She said that regardless of how bad it got, she loved getting flowers. She secretly told me that she hates to tell people to buy her flowers because she wouldn't buy them for herself. Yet, when people would ask what they could do for her, she told them to buy her flowers.

As I visited with her, she shared how she hated the smells of the hospital and chemo labs, yet if there were flowers, the aroma of the flowers would just soften the room with a refreshing smell of spring. Shelia loved resting and admiring the presence of flowers, their radiant bright colors, their heavenly beauty, the different enchanted varieties and the splendor of the flowers opening and departing. Shelia explained that even though she had so much time on her hands, she didn't feel like reading. Her eyes watered, her head hurt, and she usually tired of watching television. She found herself drawn to staring at the flowers in the bouquets nearby. Shelia loved having flowers present and received great comfort from them.

When a dear friend of hers from California sent flowers to Shelia's hospital room after surgery, she could feel her presence every time she saw and smelled the flowers. The flowers constantly wished Shelia well and encouraged her with love, comfort and support to get well, because someone loved her. Positive changes in attitudes can start the healing process. Cancer patients or patients with other serious illnesses need to be surrounded with love and encouragement through the presence of flowers, especially when individuals can't physically be there all of the time.

There is power in the flowers, given with and received. The flowers helped me to develop a positive attitude. I started seeing the beauty of the rain in the midst of the storm, not letting the cancer take me as a victim. I now was a fighter with the mental attitude of a winner. Believe it or not, I started to have more patience with the doctors and staff. Patience is a virtue whenever one experiences such severe health concerns. Some such situations are waiting for test results, being allowed limited physical activities during recoveries, undergoing initial care and patient service, waiting in doctors' offices and having patience with the medical field, family and friends. Typically, when my attitude was positive, my life felt more in harmony with my circumstances and I enjoyed conversations and fellowship with everyone who came close to me.

When my attitude changed, my perspective also changed. I noticed glimpses of blessings and felt the warmth of the sun's rays shining through the clouds of the storm. I finally felt love and support coming in; I did not feel alone; I could hear the encouraging words. I felt the sense of harmony and peace; and I was comforted knowing I was not going through this difficult circumstance without the support of God, family and friends. When I looked beyond and above the circumstances, I felt better physically, spiritually and emotionally.

Food was a great gift for my family. I was relieved of the burden of cooking and my family enjoyed the home-cooked meals. There were times during chemo treatments when my mouth, tongue and taste buds were unable to taste any flavors in food - even water didn't taste like water. I became very sensitive to the smells or the cooking of certain foods; it would cause me to feel nauseated. However, flowers were the best gift because they were for just me.

My daughter Krystle noticed the difference in my behavior and my moods when I had flowers near me. Not saying a word, Krystle got loose flowers from my flower coolers, located at my home floral business, and placed the fresh, decorative, elegant flowers in vases in a variety of places like my bedroom, kitchen, living room or the bathroom. During the summer months, Krystle picked enchanted flowers from my exquisite garden so that I could enjoy and delight in them. Having the presence of flowers accessible to me during chemo treatments helped me to focus on the delightful flowers instead of the cancer or my circumstances. The flowers introduced a positive energy of spiritual and emotional support. During all the cancer treatments, I was amazed to see and feel the ramifications of having flowers surround me during my illness and my recoveries.

Giving flowers to someone who is going through a serious illness or physical hardship will miraculously help the healing and the recovery. Patients need the presence of flowers to support and encourage the inner spirit. Honestly, I recommend giving flowers without a lot of fragrance in case the patients' senses are sensitive. Medications can cause us to become more heightened to the smells of certain foods, flowers, perfumes or candles. I recommend not using high-fragrant flowers like stargazer lilies, Casablanca lilies, jasmine, gardenias, evergreens, poet daffodils, (not all daffodils), hyacinths or lavender for cancer or very ill patients.

Medications can cause unknown reactions to any patient and certain fragrances can irritate the eyes or the nose. There are numerous flowers available with minimal fragrant aromas. Flowers influence the atmosphere and help patients focus on positive energy, rather than letting the cancer or the illness consume the patients with negative thoughts or discouraging energy. Restoration starts when a person outside of difficult circumstances can respond with positive influences to help improve attitudes and perspectives of the situation. Flowers radiate the words of encouragement to the depths of the soul, and flowers shine light into the darkness.

The Sun Shines Even When It Can't Be Seen

I have seen flowers whisper comfort to the brokenhearted and touch them with tremendous amounts of love. Tears of deep loss turn into tears of joy when they are touched with the feeling of being so loved. Something happens inside that they can't explain. The sense of warm, emotional feelings of comfort, love, and support touch the soul with every flower given to the broken.

Sometimes I have the privilege of seeing flowers speak to the broken and I watch the miraculous transformation as the tears of sadness turn to joy when they read the enclosure card with the flower arrangement. As the family reads every card, love overflows their hearts; they pause and stand in awe as the family looks deeper into the soul of the flowers and feels the heartfelt love behind the gift of the flowers. What can you say at a time like this? There is absolutely nothing that anyone can say that is comforting or encouraging.

During this difficult time, it is natural to want to express the depths of your love to the ones left behind, also sharing the loss experienced. There is nothing that can change the loss and no earthly action can make it easier. Yet the flowers whisper all the right words through silent language. Flowers touch the hearts that only the broken can feel; they comfort the spiritual soul without saying a word and heal the wounds left behind. The flowers in silence bring beauty, love, support, strength and peace in deeper inner levels of emotion that even the kindest words cannot express. During this difficult time, giving a timeless gift of flowers is one of the most effective ways to encompass someone with the feeling of being loved.

Loved ones have shared with me, "I have cried so much; how can the flowers make me cry, too?" The tears are a different kind of tears. They are the tears of joy overwhelming the feeling of loss and they become feelings of being intensely loved and honored. It is as though the hand of God touches the broken with an unfailing sense of love and a sense of having companionship during one of the loneliest moments in one's life.

How does one smile at a time like this? Yet I have seen smiles through the tears of joy warming the heart as the family admires the gift of the flowers and the sender's love. Moments like these happen all the time. Flowers can soften the hardest, toughest, strongest hearts to ultimately feel love. When one feels loved, the result is to give love back to the sender or to others. In spite of the intense feeling of loss, the broken will feel inspired to love others since they were loved. The broken will feel the love flowing through their veins, generating the will to live life in spite of their discouraging loss. Let the sun and the love shine through the darkness with the gift of a flower.

The flowers in their silent language and beauty will whisper the warmth of love and touch the souls make sure to keep. Mother Theresa once said, "See how the trees, flowers, grass—grow in silence; see the stars, the moon, and the sun, how they move in silence—we need silence to be able to touch the souls."

The Sun's Rays Melt the Frost

Have you ever noticed the sun's rays as the warmth melts the frost off the surface of everything in the landscape? Notice that the landscape behind shadows is still covered with pearly white frost. Frost needs the energy from the sun's rays to thaw the frozen crystals into dewdrops of moisture. The sun's rays melt the walls of the cold hard crystals and turn them into the receptive drops of moisture, giving blessings. Sometimes we need the sun's rays to melt some of our own crystal walls of beliefs so that we can melt the hearts of the ones we love with loving blessings.

For example, Sam grew up with the mental wall that flowers were a waste of money. Tragically, Sam got critically ill and later needed a transplant. He was transported in and out of hospitals for several months waiting unsuccessfully for a donor, as his life was failing. As the sand was falling from the hourglass, Sam's frosty crystal walls were melting. The illness was an enormous struggle mentally and emotionally for him. Yet his view on life was melting his beliefs in the world around him. Meanwhile Sam's love for his wife, Sara, grew daily and dearly. He always bought Sara nice gifts and did nice things for her. Sara knew how Sam felt about flowers and his beliefs about them being a waste of money.

For the first time, Sam, called me (I was aware of his circumstances and condition) to order flowers for Sara. When he called, I was very surprised to hear his voice because I knew of Sam's beliefs about flowers. The couple was also struggling financially with all of the medical bills. Yet the sun was melting Sam's perspectives and crystal walls and he wanted to order roses for Sara. I got all the information about the flowers, the payment, and the address for the delivery. When I asked Sam how he would like the card signed, there was a moment of silence. Then Sam hesitantly asked me how can he tell Sara how much he loves her? I reassured him that Sara would be so surprised by the flowers that this unexpected act was going to melt her heart. Sam's voice was quivering and trembling with tears as he tried to tell me what to put on the card.

Sam's heart ached in agony and despair as he tried with great anguish to keep it together being as the strong physical man that he was. The flowers were genuinely coming from a melted heart through the tears of his softened soul. The flowers were prepared without an occasion, being a gift of love. Anxiously, Sam asked me to deliver the flowers as soon as possible.

Knowing that Sara would be unsuspecting and surprised, I was anxious as I stood at the front door of their home. As the door opened, Sara admired the flowers thinking they were for Sam. In a softly spoken voice, I told Sara the flowers were for her. She paused as though she did not hear me and in disbelief glanced at the name on the enclosure card where she saw her name, "Sara." She was ecstatically surprised. She grabbed her chest with a gestured breath of air, as it took her breath away She stood a moment in disbelief as she was reaching for the enclosure card. Her hands quivered as she tried to get the envelope open quickly asking me who the flowers were from. She started to cry as she read the card out loud, "How do I tell you how much I love you? I will always love you." Sara just started to sob and smile. She knew the gift of the flowers was truly an act of love.

Sara will never forget the blessings of the heartfelt flowers or the scenario as I shared our conversation when Sam had ordered the flowers. Although the couple was going through one of the worst times in their married lives, it was the most inspirational, loving and memorable moment. There was absolute beauty in that moment, and they shared a deep love expression in that blessing. It shouldn't take a tragedy before a perspective is changed or the frosty crystal walls of life melt down. Sam has since had a successful transplant and has a healthy prognosis. Sam periodically gives Sara flowers for no special occasion, just to remind her how much he loves her.

The Son Shines Every Day

There is nothing better than planting God's seeds of love for eternal harvests of love. Everyone should send a gift of a flower anonymously as a selfless act of kindness and love for someone else. The results are phenomenal. There is an internal burst of joy that wants to explode through your veins. Your steps are a little lighter, your burdens of work are lighter, and your energy level shifts to a more productive level as a servant helping and loving others. All this enthusiastic energy comes from knowing the fact that you just brightened or touched somebody's heart and made their day better.

Giving an unexpected gift of flowers to someone is as rewarding for you as opening a gift at Christmas. When selfless acts of kindness happen, you really do open the floodgates of heavenly love. God is watching our every move and every act of kindness. Even the smallest gifts or acts are sometimes the greatest. Even if you may think no one else will notice, the most important one does. You may not see the results immediately, but do not worry you will see the seeds of love in the future. Seeds of happiness will come from what you *give!*

As flowers, we all need the sun so that we can grow and live life abundantly. The sun gives all the nourishing nutrients that the flowers need to grow and shines a beautiful radiant light that glows into the hearts of many. The sun rises dependably and loyally every day giving strength to the weak and light into the darkness. The sun is always present, above the clouds and the storms; even though I cannot see the sun, I feel the warmth of its love. The petals of the flower extend from the center much like energy radiates from the sun. Like the petals of the flower, the center of our hearts radiates love to the landscape. The sun gives the flowers energy and power to live life abundantly, blooming radiantly with our blossoms and sharing the scent of heaven for the whole world to smell.

Like a sunflower, let us turn and face the Son, choosing to live our lives searching for the energy from the Son every day of our lives. The Son shines forgiving light upon our souls, so we cannot see the shadows of darkness behind us. If we turn our eyes upon Jesus and face the Son, all of our worries will grow dim. The Son's love shines a radiant light for the whole world to see. As with the flower, there is so much about the Son worth celebrating and rejoicing.

Chapter 7
The Greatest Gift Is Love

"The greatest gift cannot be seen or touched; it must be felt through the heart." This is one of my favorite quotes by Helen Keller. Love is the greatest gift. Love cannot be seen or touched and love can only be felt through the heart. Helen was blind, yet she could see the greatest gifts that only the blind can truly see.

Flowers are always given in an expression of love. I've never seen anyone send flowers because they don't like the person or are mad at someone. Flowers are given out of genuine love and concern and to brighten someone's day, to offer a cheery get well, to say "I'm sorry, I still love you," to comfort the loss of loved ones and to celebrate birthdays, anniversaries or any other special occasions such as weddings, births and holidays.

Since my bout with breast cancer, I've come to believe that every day is a celebration of love. To me there is no better way to show love than by sending nature's paintbrushes. I've seen flowers bring so much joy and I've seen smiles on people's surprised faces or tears in their eyes as they reach out and touch their hearts.

Roses have always been beautiful and among the favorite choice for Valentine flowers. During the season, I deliver every type of arrangement from several dozen to a single stem rose. One common trait that I've noticed with all of my deliveries, not just on Valentine's Day, is that the only words that have any true meaning on the card are the sender's name. These flowers themselves always make the receiver feel special and dearly loved.

What Is Love?

Empires have been sacrificed for love. Wars have raged for love. Love has ruled mankind since the dawn of time. Today, however, love has become a word that we toss around in a pretty casual manner. We hear the word love used to describe so many different items in our lives. The word love appears in many contexts: there's maternal love, familial love, romantic love, intimate love, a wider love for fellow humans and love for God, to name but a few. Some cultures have ten or more words for different forms of love and poets and songwriters always find myriad aspects of love to celebrate.

Love is an emotion with many sides, shades, and colors. The love that we feel for parents or children is quite different from that which we feel for our sweetheart. The one is mixed with romance while the other is not. The major difference is that love is spiritual while sex is biological. Love may come and go, but there are no two love experiences that affect one in the exact same way.

There may be one love experience that leaves a deeper imprint on the heart than all others, but all love experiences are beneficial. The best definition of love that I have found is from Corinthians. "Love is patient, love is kind, it does not envy, it does not boast, it is not proud. It is not rude, it is not self seeking, it is not easily angered, it keeps no record of wrongs. Love does not delight in evil but rejoices with the truth. It always protects, always trusts, always hopes, and always preserves. Love never fails." (1 Cor. 13:4–8) (NIV). This is how God defines love. He wants us to experience it in its purest form. True love is "other-person" focused. It is giving rather than self-seeking. For us to experience this kind of love in relationships, we need to first experience God's love for us. Love is an everlasting attribute of God. He loves us unconditionally. Each time we turn our back on Him or test his love, He is there waiting for us with open arms. When we turn to God and accept His forgiveness, then we begin to experience His love.

God continues to love us no matter what we do, how we act, how we look or how much money we have. His love is not based on our physical appearance or who or what we are. His love is totally different from what society calls love. God simply tells us that His forgiveness and love is ours for the asking. It is His gift to us.

How then do we learn the true meaning of love for ourselves? First and foremost, by accepting and understanding God's love for us. Then, by insisting that we feed ourselves with that love. From this we learn how to adopt loving mindsets, feelings and behaviors. When we truly have that kind of attitude in our lives, we are increasingly a blessing to others. If you want to experience a real and meaningful love from God, then you need to open your heart to Him and allow His unconditional love to flow through you. You need to invite God, who is Love, into your heart and become filled with Him.

Love One Another

God is a show-and-tell God. The disciples witnessed the compassionate heart of Jesus—His love for each and every individual and for His Father. Loving others will demonstrate to the world that we belong to Jesus, and sharing the good news tells the world of Jesus' love. The world is watching, and we need to be accountable for our own thoughts, words, and actions. If you love Jesus, you will love others, because He loved us first.

There is a great wisdom in knowing that God is love and love is God. There is power in expressing love to one another. The greatest command is to love God with all your heart and soul. The second is to love one another as yourself. When you are expressing love you are honoring both commandments. God is always present, as love is always present. Just like the sun. You can feel the warmth of its radiant heat on your skin and in your heart. You can see with the bright light for the entire world to see. The sun is dependable and reliable as it rises every morning. We know the sun is always shining even when we can't see it and we are covered with clouds or storms.

Like the flowers, we need the sun and the rain to grow. We are alive when we can feel love and give love to others. What does the Bible say about love? "God loves us, and we should love God and love each other." How do we show our love for each other? We can send flowers as a sign of love to our family and friends. There is a certain comfort and peace in knowing that people care about us. We can show honest love for one another by looking past imperfections and seeing the beauty on the inside.

To demonstrate love, say, "I love you" with flowers. There is magic in each stem, and saying "I love you" is the most beautiful gift you can give to someone. These words are the most treasured ones that a person can hear. A blessing is not a blessing until you speak it; if you can't say the words, let the flowers speak all the right words for you.

Although it is easy to love a friend, we are also commanded to love our enemy, our opponent, someone whom we think has wronged us or our competition—in spite of how difficult it may be.

When a person shares a story about receiving flowers, his whole energy level changes. He begins to smile while telling the story; sometimes the story will even bring a tear to his eye. As if it were the moment of the greatest gift of being given a flower. It is always a positive story no matter what the occasion; it was a gift of love. The gift of flowers left footprints on the heart with a message never forgotten.

Why is it so special to give a perishable flower that will die soon? The answer is clear, flowers touch the soul, and they touch people with love. Flowers are priceless, they are worth every cent even in a poor economy. Flowers do so much for people and add value to relationships that money can't buy.

A Priceless Gift

How do we put a value on the gift of love? It has been said that "money can't buy love." Well, buying flowers can't buy love, but flowers are often given as an expression of real love. Flowers convey feelings and emotions of a loving spirit. So not only are you giving flowers, you are giving love with every gift of flowers.

I believe that when you share the gift of a flower (they are not really ours anyway—God created them like you and me), you are not only sharing and touching others with the gift of love and kindness, you are sharing and touching others with God's love. You are being the hands of Jesus, the feet of disciples. You are prophesying like the prophets and are God's almighty love and power sharing the Spirit among us.

I'll always remember all of the flowers that were sent from the heart. This book is not big enough to share them all, yet I'll try to share the story of the most impactful flowers. One story involves a dear couple named Fred and Chloe. Chloe shared with me that Fred always gave her flowers at the perfect time, when she needed them most. It was always at the right time. He wouldn't buy her flowers just because it was a holiday. For example, a couple of months after they came home with their firstborn, she was struggling with the new mom responsibilities and routines. Fred came home with a beautiful bouquet of flowers to encourage and strengthen her.

Keep your marriage young and fresh as in the earlier years; don't let the spark burn out. Keep the fire going. Fred was unexpectedly diagnosed with an aggressive cancer. Consequently, he went through numerous treatments and was struggling. Fred called me before Valentine's Day to order flowers. Fred ordered a dozen red roses for Chloe and a dozen roses for each of his two daughters-in-law. Fred ordered them knowing it was a holiday, but the price was not an issue; it was his perfect time. He ordered them because he and I knew it probably would be the last time he would send them flowers. They had to be the best. The flowers had a mission and an unforgettable message to whisper to the ones he loved.

When I asked what he would like on the cards, there was complete silence. I knew then that the flowers were going to do all the talking. Fred lost control of his emotions; with a breaking heart, he asked for a moment to get his composure back. Taking possession of the phone again, I heard Fred's voice tremble as he told me that he couldn't find the words to say. Then he asked me how to tell them how much he really loved and appreciated all they had done for him. The tears were choking his speech as he shared his heart with me. I reassured him that the flowers would whisper more to them than he could imagine; they were the perfect gift, and it was the perfect time for Fred to share his heart.

Don't wait for Valentine's Day or an anniversary to tell someone special that you love them. Anytime is a good time because none of us knows exactly how long we have left on this earth. He expressed that the words on the card and the flowers were really a gift from the heart. The flowers were genuinely coming from the heart through the tears of the softened soul. Fred also felt an inner peace as his voice was getting calmer; he was relieved by doing an act of kindness with the greatest expression of love. There is peace in the heart of a dying soul who is finally able to let his loved ones know how much he loves them.

I will tell you that as the flowers were getting designed that day, they were the most heartfelt dozens arranged on that Valentine's Day; a part of my heart was touched and given away. When the flowers were delivered no words could be shared; the surprise of the roses and who they were from did more to their hearts than he said with the words on the cards. I know they felt the tears from his heart. They were left speechless as they felt it in their hearts.

I wish he could've seen the tears of love and the way that his expression of love touched their hearts. Fred passed away a few months later. Chloe and the daughters-in-law shared with me after his funeral that they will never forget the memory and they know now how much he really did love them. The flowers whispered a deeper definition to "I love you" than those three little words could say. They felt love being expressed in their feelings, emotions, and heart.

They were also very thankful that he took the opportunity to tell and show them and took time to say goodbye before the cancer took his life. The family cannot talk about it today without tears welling up in their eyes as they remember every detail as though it were just yesterday. The memory lasts a lifetime, even though the flowers are only here for a little while. As the years go by, people will forget what you say and do, but they will never forget how you made them feel.

Not only did Fred give the greatest gift of love but he also planted the greatest seeds of love in his two sons, who were able to witness how much the flowers meant to their wives and their mom. Fred's act also expressed the importance of giving flowers now; it is the perfect time—we are all reminded how fragile life is. Fred started his generation, his son's generation and their son's generation of giving flowers. It is a beautiful legacy to leave behind and plants the seeds of love for generations to come. It was such an honor to have a hand in something so much more beautiful than the beauty of the flowers. Flowers are a reflection of God's love, beauty and grace. They are a little piece of heaven to enjoy here on earth. When we share flowers with one another, we are truly sharing the gift of God and His love for us through them.

Everlasting Love

Flowers are present in the best and worst of times. They are always present for births, weddings, celebrations, funerals, illnesses and encouragements. There really is extraordinary significance in the flowers being present on numerous occasions. They are included in some of the most special and dear moments of our lives.

If you think about it in spiritual ways, God's presence is always felt in the best and worst of times. You are never alone no matter where you are. Love is always present and you are always surrounded with love. God is the creator, and I believe there is a reason and a season for everything. If you see the beauty in the difficult and bad times, you will also see the good of every struggle.

There is such awe in the beauty and wonder of plants and nature. Every single blade of grass, every flake of snow, every single flower and every human being is just a wee bit different than anything else. There are no two things alike, you know, whether they are small, like grains of sand, or gigantic stars. All were made to be just what they are!

How foolish, then, to imitate. Each of us has a mind whose ideas and beauty never end. There will only be one of me to show what I can do, and there is only one of you as well, so you should feel very proud. There is beauty with every single flower, and wonder with every human being, as the Creator had all of this in mind. There is a season for crying and a season for laughing and dancing. There is a season for planting and a season for harvesting. Love makes everything grow. You and I are just like flowers in the garden of life. We can be the sunshine even if there is rain in the storms of life. The power is love!

God's laws are not burdensome. They can be reduced to two simple principles: love God and love others. According to Jesus, these two commandments summarize all of God's laws. Let them rule your thoughts, decisions and actions. When you are uncertain about what to do, ask yourself which course of action best demonstrates love for God and love for others. I believe that when you share the gift of flowers, you are honoring God and loving others.

Chapter 8
Now Is the Time

Now is the time to go through life pulling out the weeds while relishing in the splendor of the flowers. Many people are just passing through life almost like the main goal is to just get through it and then die, taking each breath for granted. With all the demands and responsibilities on us nowadays it's easy to see how the joys of life have somehow been demoted. Most of us feel like we don't have time to experience all that the universe has to share with us. Complacency happens in all walks of life. By the time you go to work, spend your day putting out fires, come home, eat dinner, help the kids with homework, do the dishes and get ready for bed, there isn't much time or energy left over. It is as though you're reliving the same day over and over for an eternity.

Does this sound familiar? We feel like our life has morphed into one big sacrifice. We must give up time to pay the mortgage, go to a job we don't like and spend our days doing what we think we should. This life of sacrifice isn't surprising. As parents, employees, entrepreneurs, or anyone for that matter, we're willing to give ourselves up in order to meet the needs of those closest to us. The problem is that we haven't recognized that we're actually sacrificing ourselves in the process.

What does it mean to sacrifice? It means to give up something important or valued for the sake of other considerations. We have lost the knowledge and power of knowing that we are a child of God; now only our physical part—our five physical senses—is running our lives. But we do not become happy and feel alive by just "having" more. Some of us are born knowing the connection between heaven and earth, some actively search for it, and some are thrown into it by the events and circumstances happening in their lives. But there are those who constantly live on the edge to try to find proof of a bigger purpose.

Beauty of the Morning Glory

Have you ever seen the unique beauty of a flower called a morning glory? They are beautiful garden flowers that are known for their climbing ability. The ones in my garden climb a wagon wheel and have dark green, big, beautiful, heart-shaped leaves, and they grow displaying love for the whole world to see. The blossoming flowers have some of the most unique characteristics of any flower.

I want to share the real beauty and personality of the morning glories. These fragile little flowers are the most gorgeous sky blue or ocean blue trumpet-looking flowers. The morning glory opens itself to the world in the early morning hours, in all its glory. If I look closely at its trumpet-shaped blossom, it is as though there is a beautiful light that radiates from the center to let the world see its beautiful light shine. Unfortunately, it's gorgeous, delicate, fragile life is only for one beautiful day. Although roses, tulips, geraniums, petunias and daisies bloom and last up to a couple of weeks, the morning glory lasts one day.

Jesus reminds us that we should live life like a flower, and God reminds us of how precious our life is compared to His time. We are nothing more than a vapor in the wind or the life of a flower in His time. How precious and fragile life is.

In comparison, we should live life like the flower of a morning glory; every morning we should rise and shine our beautiful light for the whole world to see no matter how long or short our life may be. We should climb whatever obstacles are in our way, and touch the world with all of our love like the heart-shaped leaves. We should radiate and live life full of joy and glory - as God looks down into His beautiful garden we are nothing more than a beautiful morning glory. Whenever I see a morning glory, I stop and admire the beauty of this beautiful flower in all its splendor, for it has touched my life, reminding me of just how fragile life is.

Did you know that the morning glory starts the day in the most gorgeous color of blue, then slowly changes, just like we go through changes? It turns to lavender and shades of violet purple toward the end of the day as the sun sets, as the morning glory's life is over and near the end. The lavenders and purples are also one of the spiritual colors of blessings in most religions. Therefore, as we grow, we should become more spiritual throughout our lives, even if it is toward the end of our lives, which is often the case for people. We should also radiate light from our blossoming life with all the love, joy and glory of praise to God in spite of whatever obstacles of life we have to climb as we change and grow nearer to God. We will bless the world around us with all the beauty we can share to brighten the world in spite of however long or short our lives may be. We should bloom wherever God plants us.

I carry a picture with me everywhere I go of a girl laughing, jumping and smiling with joy. That is how I feel. I'm so grateful to be part of God's awesome universe. My life, even when obstacles occur, is a gift that I want to open each day. When we walk with God, we are vibrant, radiant and strong. We are like enormous magnets drawing everything into our lives such as abundance, enjoyment, excitement and success. The time is now to relish every breath we take and to live life to the absolute fullest.

We have a lot to learn from flowers and about God. He did not create scarcity and limitations. In order for the pollination to work, we basically just need one type of flower with the help of a bee, but do we just have one of each? No, there are thousands and thousands of different trees, flowers, plants, species and elements. Everywhere around us there is an explosion of variety, details and color. Knowing and understanding abundance is to know that there is abundance for everyone. If you live in harmony with God you can never take more than your share. Just think about the air we breathe. He provides it for us, and we can never take more than we need because there is enough for everyone.

When we are only being, and understanding, the physical part of us thinks we are in "survival mode" thinking that we need to make sure we have enough. We want to hoard, protect and secure. Just imagine how many wars and fights have started with the desire to control water, land or resources. We have enough for everyone, but instead of having faith in God, we live by lack and limitations.

Faith

This concept of living by faith can seem really foreign with all of the negativity in the world today. Every time we turn on the news we see images of death and destruction and ruined economy, and we hear stories about people who have just given up. My motto is to never surrender. Take each day as a new beginning.

Do you remember what it's like to be in the presence of someone who is sincerely full of joy? Such people are enjoyable to be around, and they bring out the part of us that knows how to laugh. Have you experienced being around someone who knows how to savor every moment in a way that makes you want to live your life to the fullest, too? When we meet these types of individuals we walk away feeling inspired to do more with our lives. I want to inspire you to exceed all of your dreams and desires with the help of our Savior.

So, what needs to happen? You need to give yourself to God to live life to its fullest. Living in the now means filling in all those areas you've been lacking in. It all starts with awareness. With this knowledge, you can start to make conscious decisions to live in the moment. I want to point out that just because you are successful doesn't mean that you're alive. Success, money, the perfect weight and luxurious homes and cars are only temporary things. Basing your happiness on these types of items may work at first, but as time passes, you want more and more. Your Mercedes is no longer enough; you may want a Bentley. Will you be happy with more? Are you living life to the fullest? Is your life worth living?

I delivered flowers to a dear friend during the last few days of his life. I will never forget the words he shared with me. Jack grew up in poverty. He was raised on a farm in a small town in Nebraska. In spite of Jack's financial hardships, he rose up and lived a successful life, worth millions of dollars. As I was getting ready to leave, Jack called me back to his bed to tell me not to miss the moment. I paused and questioned what he meant by the 'moment'. Jack proceeded to explain that he wished he had invested as much time and energy in accumulating relationships as he invested in accumulating houses. Relationships are the real gems of life—they make a life worth living and are the things that matter the most! Relationships with our friends and family should be our highest priority in life. It's not things that matter the most; it's the relationships I have with people that matter the most!

Don't miss the moments in your life when you can invest your time, money, gifts and things, with people to enrich your relationships, rather than investing in accumulating things or stuff. Jack did not have a lot of friends or family near him during the last few days of his life. But he truly treasured the few friends and family who sent flowers to enrich his soul. He realized that the greatest gifts were not seen in the stuff but in the unseen things.

Take a moment to observe where you place your values in life. Examine and evaluate your calendar, checking account, and your gifts and talents. Because where you deposit your time, money, and resources is a reflection of what you consider to be most valuable. Where do you spend your time? Are you depositing time into the things in life of value or in the people you love? Where, who, or what do you spend your money on? Who, where, or what do you share your gifts and talents with?

What's really important? There is a great benefit in this economic recession because it helps us to focus on what really is important to us. The recession forces us to determine the importance of our values and investments. My wish is that we stay sober in this economic weather and stay focused on the real values in our investments for the rest of our lives. We need to stay true to our relationships and add value to them. Giving from our hearts is more important than what is in our wallet. What's really important? Don't miss the opportunities in your life to truly live life abundantly.

Love Now

I'll never forget this story because it touched my heart, as I know it will yours. I was delivering a funeral arrangement to the mortuary for viewing or visitation prior to the funeral. Ken, the funeral director, was passing through the lobby and greeted me. Ken was short handed with his working staff, and he asked me if I would take care of the flowers, as he needed to be with another family. I'm like family or one of the staff, so, knowing the procedures and the facility, I was comfortable helping him out.

While Ken escorted me to the visitation room on the way to the other family needing his service, he told me that the husband was in the room visiting his wife. I expected the husband to be grief stricken and even more so due to the tragic circumstances. My heart was already feeling compassion for this man whom I had never met. When Ken shared with me that the husband was in the visiting room with her, I was already trying to prepare myself. What would I say if I had to say anything? What could I say?

When I stepped in the room, even as a florist, I was taken away by all the roses in the room. I did not even notice the husband. The room was simply gorgeous. The aroma of the room was so fragrant; it was as though you had stepped into heaven's gates, with the overwhelming beauty and the smell of fresh roses. There were roses of every color. There were dozens of roses in different shades of yellows, reds, corals, pinks, whites and lavenders. There were roses of every color in groupings of beautiful bouquets and sprays. I had never seen so many roses or flowers for one funeral. The roses filled the room and it was absolutely exquisite. Words just can't possibly describe the beauty or capture the moment. Close your eyes and try to imagine for yourself the beauty and make yourself present in the room so you can truly feel and smell the atmosphere of this beautiful moment.

I just stood in awe, speechless. I took a minute to admire all the beauty of this moment and smell the roses. I saw the husband weeping in a chair beside the casket. When the husband noticed me in the room, he started blowing his nose, wiping his tears with his handkerchief and trying to pull himself together. I stepped very quietly in the process of getting a floral stand from behind the curtain to place the flowers I was delivering on a stand to display amongst all the sprays of roses.

Like I said, I was so taken away that I just took a moment and stood in awe and admired the room. It seemed this lady was so dearly loved. The middle- to later-aged husband questioned me as he stood up and asked me if I was a florist and I told him that I was. All I could think of at the time was to tell him how beautiful all the roses were in the room; as a florist, I had never seen anything that was as beautiful as this was.

My heart and words were compassionate as I consoled him and told him how I couldn't imagine what he was going through. Pausing a moment, I sincerely added, that I could tell how much he loved her.

He brokenly replied how much he did love her and after a moment of silence, he told me how much his wife loved roses. With my whole heart, I just knew that the story behind whatever he was going to tell me would make me cry. He then told me that his wife always wanted him to buy her roses, but he never did. The tears ran down both our faces. I was not prepared for his response of "I never did." It echoed in my mind, my heart and my soul. I was speechless and numb. My heart just broke for him. I suddenly realized how much he really did love her, and yet the extreme amount of pain in his eyes told of regret, a heavy burden of a broken heart of guilt. With depths of regret he wanted to tell her and show her how much he really did love her through all of the beautiful roses.

The roses then took on a whole new perspective. I realized how much deeper his suffering and loss was than it had first appeared. All I could do was to gently wrap my arms around him as we both cried. He explained to me how much he loved his wife and regretted thinking, "Someday I'll buy her a rose when I have more time." He shared again, with deep regrets, how much she loved roses and I reassured him that his wife knew how much he loved her. He looked at me with brokenness, hurt and sorrow and as though he were pleading and begging me to tell more people to not wait to send flowers, because you may not get another chance.

He told me how much flowers mean to people, and how I need to change men like himself and change people's perspective on buying flowers. I reassured him that his living testimony was worth more and would be more impactful than my words coming from a florist. What was in his heart was the true heart of giving the gift of a flower. As I reassured him that he could be a living testimony, he told me how embarrassed and ashamed he was to admit to anybody that he never bought his wife a rose. He truly did not want anyone else to make the same mistake he did. Sadly, he was too embarrassed and ashamed to share it with anyone else.

I was so touched that he shared and opened up to me, a complete stranger. We visited for quite a while without interruption, and I comforted him with forgiving encouragement. Confiding in me, he had released a heavy burden and a peaceful spirit was being released. For no rhyme or reason, in that moment, this man shared his innermost thoughts with me.

Reflecting in the timeless moments that I shared with a stranger and remembering the unforgettable compassion of this man's eyes and heart, I knew there was a reason his life was shared with me. This moment inspired me to want to share his story and educate people about the indescribable impact and inspiration that flowers truly give people. His story taught me that there is no perfect time and the only time we have is right now.

Have you ever had someone close die without warning and wished you had expressed how much you loved them? People live as though they're going to live forever. However the truth is that we are all going to die someday and we usually have no idea when it is going to happen. Intellectually, we all know that we will die but hardly anyone lives life that way. We put off telling our loved ones how much they mean to us all the time. Or we wait to treat them to something special because we "can't afford it."

Is there a loved one right now whom you want to tell how much you love them? Perhaps you don't want to just say the words but would like to actually express the love language through the silence or whisper of flowers to the heart. Cherish the time you have. Live your life in the moment. None of us know how much time we have left, so make the most of it. "Forget me not" is in the silence of everyone's heart. Give your loved ones a flower today.

God will speak to you in a whisper. He speaks to the selfless not the self seeking. The first step is to learn how to be silent, aware, and attuned to the whisper of God. He doesn't always speak in a mighty roar of a loud thunder, or in the power of all consuming fire. His heart is full of love and compassion. What is God whispering to you? I hope you'll listen to the stillness of the whisper.

Now, take a moment and sit in a quiet place. Find your inner voice and listen to it. Take a moment and be quiet. What has the little voice in your head been saying? Are you inspired? Have you been living according to what others think and want? Do you feel that something is missing in your life? Do you need to be rejuvenated? When was the last time you took time for yourself? You intuitively know what feeds you.

We can have a new lease on life and accomplish things for our friends and family and invest in our relationships. Say no to guilt and fear. You have the right to live a happy, full and abundant life.

Chapter 9
Gratitude

There is so much beauty in this world. Some mornings I take my cup of coffee and sit outside just to enjoy God's splendor. The sounds of the wind whistling through the trees, the songs of the meadow larks, the clouds in the sky, the flowers in my garden and all of the wonders and beauty of nature overwhelm me.

I enjoy watching my dogs run and play. I take time to reflect on how much my family and friends mean to me and how I can improve my life. This time allows me to let gratitude flow throughout my body. After my bout with cancer, I truly appreciate what I have, and I make every effort to not take anything in life for granted. When you think your life is over, it is amazing how your outlook changes. What was once taken for granted is now valued beyond belief. Sometimes we all need time to run away from the reality of the distraction that is happening in life.

Having an attitude of gratitude, or appreciating what you have and being thankful, will actually bring more into your life.

I know this is the case for me. Keep in mind, I'm not telling you to settle for what you have but to strive to grow toward the sun. While you're growing, be thankful for all that you encounter along your journey. Yes, that includes the bad too. Offerings of praise and gratitude to God is true honor and worship for God. Gratitude increases what you have in life because it allows you to truly see all that you have. It allows your mind to focus on what you have instead of what you don't have.

Showing appreciation and gratitude to someone is a great way to celebrate your life. If you consciously look at what you do have and are truly thankful for it, you are admitting that God has blessed you! You may be thinking to yourself right now, "How big of a difference can it make in my life if I'm thankful for every little thing in life?" You may even think that "Saying 'thank you' certainly can't change my circumstances." I know for a fact that it can. You see, God created our minds and gave us the freedom to think whatever thoughts we choose to think. At this very moment, you can let Satan creep in and trick you into thinking about how bad your life is, or you can thank God for all that He has given you in your life. You can think about whatever you want to think about!

God designed our minds in such a way that what we consistently focus on is what we will bring into our lives. For me, when I had cancer, I didn't focus on pain and death; instead I concentrated on healing, watching my children grow, and growing old with Kevin. Stop for a moment and think about an event in your life and how your thoughts affected the outcome. I'm sure you know people who are consistently negative. Their main focus is how bad everything in their life is, and as a result, they are chronic complainers. God tells us to minister to those who are in need. I say when you encounter this type of a person you should counteract each negative word with a positive one. Set an example for them, and show them through your gratitude that they should be thankful for all that they have instead of concentrating on what they lack.

You are a product of your own thoughts that you have built into your heart. Once you choose to be grateful, you'll notice that all of your thoughts will follow suit. Give God the appreciation He so deserves and show gratitude for what He has blessed you with. By giving your time, tithes, worship and praise of gratitude to God, you'll see more of His blessings in your life.

The Eternal Promise

From the air I breathe to the food I eat, to the ability to use my hands to create beautiful floral arrangements, I am eternally grateful. God increases His blessings on those who are grateful. For example, God granted me a healthy recovery and more strength than I had before cancer. He bestows even more knowledge and prosperity to those who are grateful for their knowledge or wealth. This is because they are sincere people who are contented with what God gives and are pleased with the blessings; they take God as their friend. Showing gratitude is also a sign of our closeness to and love of God. Having a love for God is one of the greatest motivators for living for God. People who give thanks have the insight and capability to perceive the beauties and blessings that God creates, such as flowers.

True believers who remain grateful to God even during the most difficult trials reap the best rewards. Again, my remission from cancer is an excellent example. Those who are able to perceive the good aspect of every event and situation see goodness in this, too. For example, God states that He will test people with fear, hunger, loss of wealth or life. In such a situation, we need to not only show gratitude but rejoice that God trusts us enough to handle such tribulations. Know that when you have gratitude, God rewards you with the gifts of blessings in return for the steadfastness you displayed in this test.

The wisest words, we can ever speak, are the words we share as a witness to God through the living testimonies of our life experiences. Every life experience from hardships to joy is an opportunity to know God better, as we grow and trust him more. God does not impose on anyone more than they can bear. The steadfastness and submission of such awareness leads us to patience and gratitude. Therefore, it is an obvious attribute of believers to show unwavering dedication and submission, and God promises to expand His blessings on His grateful servants both in this world and in the hereafter.

As Christians, we can and will receive blessings and abundance from God. Why? Because God promised us that we will receive blessings and abundance. God always keeps His promises. In today's tumultuous times, it seems more than ever that family relationships have become strained to the breaking point and that many external forces are at work against us. In any newspaper, you'll read about the mismanagement of resources, failing businesses, fraudulent people, scams and scandals. Family relationships are strained with the rising numbers of divorces in our society and addictions to substances like alcohol or drugs. We need to realize that this constant state of wanting more and more of worldly obsessions without taking the time to show gratitude for what blessings we do have is partly to blame.

People have become lazy in work ethics, blaming others for their own misfortune; they have become chronic complainers with an attitude for a handout. People are accountable for their own environment as much or little as they accept it as the truth of their reality. Satan can work his way in and trick us into wanting more. His lies wrap themselves around our soul and create a craving for more worldly possessions. It's easy to fall prey to Satan's ways.

What is the difference between the people who thrive and the ones who just endure? Gratitude. An attitude of gratitude separates the winners from the losers. Those who never try fall beside the road and are trampled by those who are willing to thank God and give Him all of the glory. The act of not trying is a sin in itself because it is an act of defeat, and God is not a defeatist.

I depend on God and seek His trust through gratitude. I know that He will always be there for me in any problem, big or small. You wouldn't dream of accepting a gift from a close friend and not say thank you, so why in the world do so many of us take all of God's gifts without giving Him a daily dose of gratitude?

We need to show God thanks and be grateful for all that He has given us. With an attitude of gratitude, you become more at peace and even a bit more confident, for you know that you have all that you need in life. Once you incorporate the practice of gratitude in your life, you will have the capability of becoming a person whom everyone respects for your ability to grab everyone's attention each time you enter a room. You will hold your head up a little higher, walk a little brisker and set the tone for the conversation. Your confidence will be that of a person who is at peace. People will gravitate to you, hoping that some measure of what you have will rub off on them.

What an amazing God we serve. Through His word we have been given all that we need in this world. I want to take a moment and point out some promises God made to us through His word, especially for those of you who are going through trials in your life and are having a difficult time showing gratitude. Take a look at the following and think about how often you say thank you to Him.

Finances. We've gone through several trials and tribulations in our finances over the years. At one point, we thought we were going to lose our home, but my husband and I stayed in a constant state of gratitude and our prayers have been answered.

Health. With my cancer, I read Bible verses repeatedly. I never once lost faith in God and was grateful for Him walking by my side every step of the way.

Purpose. God's purpose for me was to write this book and share my story with you. I hope that my words of encouragement have inspired you to bring the beauty of flowers into your life and take the next step necessary to move you closer to God.

Our thoughts are nothing more than what we choose them to be. It is God's destiny for you to be happy and live a life of blessings. God has supplied you with abundance, and you should show Him your gratitude. Saying thank you takes little effort yet it has lasting effect. Tell God how grateful you are to be in His hands.

Our loving God has made us an eternal promise of salvation, and we should be forever grateful. He loves each and every one of us more than we will ever know. Recognize, appreciate and be thankful for everything that you have at this moment! Be grateful to God for all that you have and continue to look to Him to supply all that you need! Every person is in need of God at every instant of life. If the promise does not come right away, be patient and rest assured that God fulfills all promises, which is why gratitude is so important!

Make Gratitude a Daily Practice

When most people sit down to dinner, they express gratitude for the heaping plate of food before them. Some people's grace is genuinely offered to God in heartfelt prayers, but others' words are offered in a cursory manner. It seems as though we, me included at times, focus more on the food on the plate than on the words of thanks to God. It's easy to find ourselves feeling physically full but spiritually empty at the end of dinner because so many of us don't make a conscious effort to include God in our words of gratitude. We need to make a conscious effort to feed ourselves the physical food of bread as well as fill ourselves with the spiritual bread of Jesus.

So the question is, how do we make gratitude a daily practice without it turning into a robotic action? We need to look at the bigger picture. So many of us forget to factor in how God had a hand in everything in our life. Many people don't realize that all of their gifts are from God. Many people instead believe that they acquire everything by their own efforts. This is in gratitude toward God.

I find it amazing that people will say thank you to a person whom they've never met and will probably never see again in their life for doing something as small as holding a door open, yet spend all their lives ignoring the countless blessings that God gives them. If you tried to number God's blessings, you could never count them. God is ever forgiving and most merciful with His grace. I make a constant effort to be aware of my weaknesses and, in humility before God, render thanks to Him for every blessing granted. Wealth and possessions are not the only blessings for which I thank God. He is owner of all that we have; I express my inner gratefulness for good health, success, knowledge, wisdom, love of faith, and understanding, insight, foresight and for power. I am thankful for being rightly guided and for being in the company of believers. All of our blessings should make us immediately turn to God, express our gratefulness to Him, and reflect on His mercy and compassion.

Earlier we discussed taking responsibility for our thoughts, and we need to make a conscious effort to make gratitude a priority in our life. With a little thought and planning, we can transform empty words of thanks into meaningful and spirit-filled gratitude. We need to not only have a belief in God but also a desire to have Him in every aspect of our lives. If we possess these we are well on the way to creating a daily habit of gratitude. Below, I'm going to share with you the four steps that I take daily to keep gratitude alive in my heart.

- **Open the Door.** Let God in your heart. You have to have courage to experience God. I relate this to a flower delivery I once made. We live in a small town, so I pretty much know everyone there. I had a delivery to this lady who was a wee bit quirky. She was scared to answer the door and didn't like to talk to people. I carried up a beautiful bouquet of lilies for an Easter delivery and rang the doorbell. I knew she was home, but she wouldn't open the door. So I had no other choice but to take the bouquet back to the shop and call the sender to come pick it up. The same is true with letting God in your heart. If you are too afraid to open the door, you may miss out on a wonderful experience.

- **Acknowledge what you are grateful for.** I say all that I'm grateful for each morning while I'm drinking my coffee. If you're uncomfortable speaking out loud, keep a gratitude journal. Write down at least one thing each night that you're thankful for. No matter how you acknowledge your gratitude with praise and worship, make sure that it is done with purposeful intention and direct it toward God. Imagine that you're inviting God into your thanksgiving. Remember, if you don't invite God into experience, He may not know to show up.

- **Keep the faith.** You have to have a strong faith in God. First, believe in God, and second, have faith that you can have an experience of gratitude with Him. Faith is daring the soul to see beyond what the eye can see.

- **Find a special place and time.** My special place is our patio or our bedroom. Your sanctuary can be anywhere you like. This is a quiet space in which you can spend some time alone in contemplation with God. When you make the effort to create a sacred space and time you will experience His presence as a peaceful spiritual atmosphere that fills your heart with more energy.

By taking these four steps toward a meaningful and spiritual expression of gratitude toward God, you'll feel at peace and will be spiritually enriched.

Show Gratitude with Flowers

Why is it that we don't show our affection and devotion to the ones we care about until a loved one is gone? I don't believe it has to be that way. There are numerous ways in which we can tell people how grateful we are for them being in our lives. To me, the obvious way to thank someone is with flowers. Flowers can be given "just because" or simply to show that you care. As simples as it may be; Fred always sends flowers to his mom on his birthday, with a heart of gratitude for his loving mom giving life to him, and thanking her for all her sacrifices being a wonderful mom. It is a great idea, and a beautiful way to express gratitude for your mom, on Mothers Day, her birthday, holidays or anytime.

Flowers are a wonderful gratitude gift to convey how much we appreciate the loved ones in our lives.

Saying thank you with flowers is appreciated by the receiver. Whether it's a dozen roses, a single flower, flowers of different varieties or a handpicked garden flower, it is certain to brighten someone's day. I offer a wide selection of floral arrangements, and I make sure that the freshest flowers are sent to my clients every time. When thank you buds are sent, the receiver has the pleasure of watching one of God's masterpieces bloom.

Thank you arrangements can be fun and frilly, romantic and intimate, friendly and playful. But whatever the mood, you will always hit the right note with these wonderful petals of gratitude. If you are uncertain as to what flowers will best state how you feel, don't fret; you cannot make a mistake.

Don't wait to let the people you love know how grateful you are to have them in your life. Send them a bright and vibrant colorful bouquet of flowers. Flowers have been such a huge part of my life and I feel a sense of gratitude with each one I touch. If you are lifting other people up, you are raising other people up to become more valueable. Sharing gratitude is the best means for a membership drive to achieve our spiritual goal. I truly believe that through gratitude our world can become a better place. We cannot underestimate the power of gratitude and tapping into the hearts of the people to help them experience gratitude as well.

When was the last time you said thank you? When was the last time you wrote a note to someone and expressed how much you appreciate them? When was the last time you called somebody and told them how much they mean to you? When the expression of gratitude is released, you begin to live life fully by living life thankfully.

There is magic in those two little words: "Thank you."

When you say thank you with flowers it is as though a magic dust were sprinkled on your relationship. In tough economic times it is even more critical to not just have a business relationship but a heartfelt relationship. Nobody cares how much you know until they know how much you care. When you care for someone you not only enrich his or her life, you enrich yourself. In spite of the number of competitors, your client will remain loyal to you and will sustain you through the tough times.

The businesses that give back to their loyal customers will be rewarded with a better return than all the money spent in advertising for new customers. The key for a successful business is taking care of your loyal clients and caring for people. Giving flowers to your clients, employees and friends, is the best advertisement that a business or friend can share. You not only build a better business, you have also invested in building a better relationship. The corporate accounts from doctors, banks, realtors, dentists, churches, mechanics, tire stores and many other businesses that give flowers have a huge number of loyal customers who return and increase sales. When flowers have been given, I've seen a difference in the working atmosphere; employees work a little harder, are more dependable, have better attitudes, work in harmony with fellow employees and, work diligently for the company. Customers respond with more loyalty and have a better attitude and patience while doing business with the company. Investing in flowers for your business relationships is worth more than all the money spent on advertising or personal knickknacks.

In my experience, the businesses that have regular floral accounts are very successful and their businesses are not affected by the economy. The tire stores that give a single carnation to all of their customers or just to the ladies, believe it or not, have higher sales than the tire shops that don't give flowers. The realtor that sends a housewarming plant or flowers of some kind will usually receive loyal service when they are ready to sell the home or buy a new one. The banks, doctors and dentists that send flowers to fellow employees or customers when they are ill or lose a loved one will reap the rewards with the results of increased net worth.

Zig Zigler once said, "If and when you add value to others, you add value to the relationship and are raising them up to a higher level. Egos let go when the leaders know, care, and understand other people's values. You will raise others up to a higher level."

If a company invests not only in its customers but also in its staff, it will have a better working relationship and the turnover of new employees will be dramatically less. All because the flowers made your staff or employee feel special and appreciated. For a business there is less turnover when there is harmony in the atmosphere. It costs a business in production and success when it has to hire and train new employees.

The flowers really do whisper the words that the business sometimes neglects to say on a daily basis. When the opportunity arises, it is the business's responsibility to reach out and inspire the individuals to be all they can be. The flowers whisper, "You are special; you do make a difference. We appreciate you; we miss you; you help the team be a better team of service and working together. We care about you. In sympathy, caring hearts are there for you.

When the employee returns, from a leave of absence and received a flower or a plant during the absence they have more energy, a desire to work harder and have fewer sick days. They are more efficient and many personal conflicts between fellow employees disappear. I have always said that we are not here to compete with each other; we are here to complete each other. We are not just placed here on this earth to see through one another but to see one another through. There is more harmony and a peaceful working environment. The number one result is a positive and better attitude overall with the company and fellow employees.

All successful companies have a great team; it takes a great team to have a successful business. You can't have one without the other. Helen Keller once said "Alone we can do so little; together we can do so much more. "It is not a secret that flowers really do have a significant role in the corporate business world. If you have never tried it, I dare you to do it, and you will see the phenomenal results in the net worth of the business an in the relationships with your employees, vendors, and clients. It will be worth giving flowers, because the return is much greater than the cost of the floral gift.

Over my 30 years in the floral business, I have witnessed the difference between the businesses and the people who do send flowers and the ones who don't. Lots of people and businesses come and go. Yet the ones who do the little extra stand above the rest; they are still very strong and successful, no matter what the economy is, or who the president is. The economy has no effect on a great foundation of good relationships in business with clients or staff or in personal relationships with friends and family.

Not only am I speaking to the CEOs and owners, I'm also sharing this wisdom with the employees and staff. The responsibility also goes for a good employee or staff member. The boss has a very stressful job and a huge responsibility and usually makes more sacrifices than one is aware of (at least the truly goodhearted bosses do). The thought and care exhibited by employees through the gift of flowers can be very powerful.

A married couple owned and operated a small restaurant in our town. The wife, Betty, had some serious health concerns. The employees sent the owner's wife some flowers in the hospital. The husband, Adam, was very touched by his employees' caring concern. Adam's outlook was influenced by the act of kindness. Adam shared that it was the first time he felt like his crew of employees really cared about them personally, not just their paycheck.

There was a sense of family relationships and responsibilities building among the crew. When his wife passed away it was extremely difficult for him, and his employees sent flowers in memory of his wife. When Adam saw the arrangement in memory of her life, he was captivated by the love in the flowers. The flowers were in Betty's favorite colors; they were her favorite flowers, her favorite coffee cup, silverware and napkins with an accent of butterflies. She loved butterflies and she always rolled the silverware for the restaurant.

Flowers express so much more when you to add personality and character with special touches. The flowers are even more alive and expressive with personality. Adam was so touched by the act of kindness and support. He shared that he will never forget the flowers, and he can still picture the arrangement as though it were yesterday. What a beautiful memory to hold on to; the flowers whispered more in their silence than one will ever know.

As the owner, he shared with me that even though his wife was gone, the love he felt from his crew gave him the strength and the desire to keep the business (instead of selling) and focus on his staff, because now they had become his family and that is where his heart is.

To this day, the business is a very successful restaurant with the same cooks, waiters and waitresses. It is a wonderful place to enjoy dinner when the working atmosphere feels like family. Not only that—the staff all share that Adam is a great boss, even though they know that they could probably work somewhere else and get paid more. They are completely satisfied because of the relationship and environment. When the business makes money, Adam gives bonuses of money to the staff in appreciation. He gives flowers to his staff and customers in times of illness and death. Adam is now a loyal floral customer with an open account.

It is so important to show your boss how much he is loved and appreciated! It is not brownnosing; the boss is worth the investment of showing appreciation. One will see the results immediately in a better attitude from the boss and a desire to take better care of the employees or staff. The boss will make better decisions for the staff support them. The boss in a highly stressful job will talk and communicate with a respectful and honorable presence. It helps to build a relationship rather than walls in any business.

As a business owner myself, if you are a business owner (it does not matter what kind of business), you *need* to invest in relationships now more than ever. The key is investing in the relationships that you can build; it's the relationships that will survive the economic weather. Flowers are the perfect way to express the message that you care for your staff, employees, boss or clients—each and every one is important for harmony. We cannot do anything alone without the help of others supporting us. Investing in relationships can be as simple as saying "Thank you" and appreciating the ones around you. Do it and say it more often, and you will make a difference in the ones around you.

Touch of Faith

Flowers can touch the lives of everyone in the church community or congregation. If you are involved with a church, see if they have a program or a service to send flowers to the shut-ins or hospital. If not, you can be the feet of Jesus and the hands of God and start a mission to serve as a servant helping others in their times of need.

It does not matter whether the church community is large or small; what is important is the relationship with members of the church and the community around the church. People remember who was there during the difficult times; they will never forget the ones who were there, and they have a hard time forgiving the ones who were not there. Humans, Jesus said, are only human in nature, and people will be human with selfish emotions. Even the strongest of faiths will fall short of earthly emotions.

God wants to use you and the church to touch people with flowers in their times of need or celebration. Churches that have a program or mission set up have stronger relationships in the church and the community, as though it were a family. After all, we are one family under God. Churches that don't have a service set up to help others through the giving of flowers are suffering financially and in membership. I want to encourage you and your church to invest in building relationships with one another now more than ever. Hope and grace are being squashed with the overwhelming fears of uncertainty, poverty, security, and troubled times. Mother Theresa shared "There is more hunger for love and appreciation in this world, than for bread." During these troubled times, we are to rise up and help others in times of need; we should love each other and build relationships, because God wants a relationship with each and every one of us. It's not the religion that will save and help people - it is the relationship with Him that will save us.

Touch people by healing, comforting, encouraging, strengthening, giving, and loving others. Miracles happen when someone is touched by faith and has the faith to believe that anything is possible with God. When someone receives flowers from a church or members of the church, he will feel the sense of God's love. He will feel the love and support from an extended family and will be encouraged that others care. This usually results in appreciation with more active membership, increased financial giving, loyalty to church fellowships, increased involvement and giving of oneself for others. Touch someone with faith through the gift of flowers because you care and because God cares.

Chapter 10
Lasting Legacy

One of my missions in life is helping to spread God's word, especially to those who don't know Him, and to teach women about breast cancer awareness through my Breast Friends Breast Cancer Support Group non profit organization. I am forever grateful that God has given me the courage and strength to do both.

Make this life of yours into a work of art. Your life's presence will be summed up in a few words—let those words be good and true. Remember, they will talk about you when you are gone. We only live once, but once is enough if we do it right. Live your life in a Christ-like manner with class, dignity and style, so that an exclamation mark, rather than a question mark, signifies it! So what legacy awaits you? When you take your final bow, who will you be? How will you enter eternity? Will you be just a footnote in history?

Robert Frost, the famous American poet, once wrote, "Two roads diverged in a wood, and I took the one less traveled by, and that has made all the difference." So I decided to write to help Breast Friends and write *Flowers Whisper* to give people a gift of hope and to encourage them to love one another. There is no such thing as fear and insecurity.

When I found out that I had breast cancer, I was scared; there was no guarantee of a cure. Many people spend a good portion of their lives doing something that they don't enjoy for work. Why? For money? What good is money if there is no time to spend it? What good is time if we cannot enjoy it? The crazy thing is that we can all follow our dreams; however, most people have excuses that are way too good to give up in pursuit of a dream!

How hard we will try to defend our mistakes and excuses only to have a better way lying right before our eyes? Don't let the fear of taking risks take you off your path. There are many dangers that cannot be prevented, even with helmets, bulletproof vests and seat belts. Contracts are only as good as the paper they are written on. All of us face risks, seen and unseen, in everyday situations. Confronting life's risks will challenge you at many different times in your life. But how do you know if the risk you are engaging in is worth it? How do you confront actual and potential risks?

Rose

Her name was Rose, and red roses were her favorite. Every year her husband sent red roses tied with pretty red bows on Valentine's Day. The year he died, the roses were delivered to her door like they had been all the years before, with a card saying, "Be my Valentine." Each year, he sent a card saying, "I love you more this year than I did last year on this day. My love for you will always grow, with every passing year." Rose knew this was the last time that the roses would be delivered. She figured that her husband had ordered roses in advance, before he had died. Her loving husband did not know that he would pass away first. He always liked doing things early, way before the time. That way, if he got too busy, everything would work out fine.

Rose trimmed the stems and placed them in a very special vase. Then she set the vase beside her favorite portrait of her loving husband's smiling face. She enjoyed sitting in the presence of the roses and her husband's portrait. A year went by and it was hard to live without her best friend; loneliness and solitude consumed her emotions. On Valentine's Day, the doorbell rang, and there were roses, sitting by her door.

Rose brought the roses in and then just looked at them in shock. Then she went to the telephone to call the florist shop. The owner answered and she asked him if he would explain why someone would do this to her causing her such pain. The owner told Rose that her husband always planned ahead; he left nothing to chance. There was a standing order on file in the shop for Rose paid in advance by her husband. Rose thanked him and hung up the phone, her tears now flowing, her fingers trembling as she slowly opened the card. Inside the card, she saw that he had written her a note in his handwriting, in the silence; this is what he wrote ...

Hello, my love, I know it's been a year since I've been gone. I hope it has not been too hard for you. I know it must be lonely, and the pain is very real, for if it were the other way around, I know how I would feel. The love we shared made everything so beautiful in life. I loved you more than words can say. You were the perfect wife; you were my friend and lover, and you fulfilled my every need. I know it's only been a year, but please try not to grieve; I want you to be happy. That is why the roses will be sent to you for years. When you get these roses, think of all the happiness that we shared together, and how both of us were blessed. I have always loved you and I know I always will. But, my love, you must go on and keep living; please find happiness in some way. The roses will come every year, and they will only stop when the door is not answered. The florist will come three times that day, in case you have gone out. After his last visit, he will know to take the roses to the place where I've instructed him and place the roses where we are together once again. My Rose, my love will always grow more for you with every passing year 'til we are together once again. Red roses will always be my favorite rose for the Rose of my life.

Making a Difference

For a few months before I found out I had cancer, I struggled with these warts on my left wrist and arm. We treated them, froze them and then burned them with acid which actually gave me second degree burns on my wrist. The warts still persevered through the scar tissue. The dermatologist one day just asked me point blank if I had cancer. I told her "no" and she explained to me that warts are just a virus, and something more severe was going on somewhere else in my body. She warned me to be aware of any lumps, chronic headaches, abnormal bowel movements or anything.

Six months later, my husband noticed a lump in my breast. During my mammogram, they came in to take more pictures and said the doctor would call me soon. The biopsy was positive. I was diagnosed in August, 2003, two days before I was to leave on a mission trip to San Diego, California with my daughter as the chaperon driver for our church youth mission trip. after positive. Perfect timing - two days before the mission trip, God was able to minister to me the words I needed to hear and the courage to endure the journey that I was about to take. In Kings 8:24(NKJV) it says, "If God brings it to you—God will bring you through it"; that was encouraging for me to focus on. I'm a breast cancer survivor. The pastor, my daughter, my best friend (chaperoning also) and I were the only ones who really knew. I did not want the trip to be about me; it was for a bigger mission. It was incredible how God encouraged me through the mission, the children and other mission people who did not know. It was then that I learned I was not going to go through this alone; He was going to be there every step of the way. God knows every detail and has divine timing. God orchestrates every moment, sees everything and knows and plans everything. I went on the mission trip to San Diego, and came home. The following weekend, Kevin and I enjoyed celebrating our 20th class reunion with dear friends before I had surgery.

After surgery, I had a month of tests, decisions and events I had a double mastectomy; one side was more radical than the other side. The doctor said the cancer mass was more on my chest wall; it was shaped like a pear. The small portion, which my husband noticed wasn't a normal lump texture, was just the tip of the mass. The larger mass was on my chest wall and could not be felt by physical touch. I had a lot of lymph node involvement, so they were worried that it had spread to my bones and metastasized to my main organs. I went through more tests. They found a spot on my kidney, but not on any bones yet. So they proceeded to get very aggressive with chemo treatments.

I was so severely sick that a dear friend would come home with me from my chemo treatments with an open line to keep fluid and anti nausea medicine in me, but nothing really helped. I was so sick every time. The last chemo treatments made my bones ache severely with pain. I felt that if the cancer didn't kill me, the chemo would. Yet I survived! I had six weeks of radiation. After that, all my cells and body would get back to normal, and then I could proceed with the reconstruction of my breasts. The doctor shared with me that he wasn't sure the chemo would work. I told him that I had so much more I wanted to share and do and be; that I was willing to fight and do whatever I needed to do, and there were going to be many prayers.

Today he still reminds me that I'm a walking miracle. So now you know—who really was the great physician? I am cancer free today. During my cancer, I was truly so blessed to have close family, dear friends and wonderful support from the church and community, as I shared with my precious mom in the floral business in Windsor. Word got out to Tracy and Stephanie who were also victims of breast cancer. They had been diagnosed in the spring of 2003. Somehow we connected. Through our experiences, we became "Breast Friends"; we helped each other and shared encouragement, tips, foods and alternative remedies to chemo side effects. After going once to a cancer support group at the local hospital, I didn't return. I was terribly discouraged and disappointed.

My friends and family were more of a support to me than the cancer support at the hospital was. My "breast friends", Tracy and Stephanie, became so close during the treatments that we decided we still needed a reason to stay in touch. We were so blessed to have each other and our support groups, family, etc. and knew there were other women not so fortunate. We decided to see if there were otherwomen who needed emotional support that we could connect with. We publicly announced a breast cancer support meeting in a local church.

We started having more of a true financial and emotional need for the town for this kind of support. Now the surrounding towns, Greely, Loveland and Ft. Collins, as well as the American Cancer Society, recommend that women come see us. We have about 55 women; we have lost some of our friends. Yet I have received so much more. The women become like sisters; we share some very personal difficult moments. We are a great source for wisdom and knowledge and comfort that a doctor or a brochure cannot touch. We started helping women out of our own broke pockets and decided that we should see if the community would help us and they did. We were so blessed to have their financial support. We have been so surprised by the number of women who have continued to support the organization. Our personal finances from our previous experiences and responsibilities were already stretched.

We formed a 501C3 nonprofit organization called "Breast Friends Breast Cancer Support Group Foundation." We make turbans, help with wigs, make meals and heart pillows after surgery, provide escorts to doctors, do house cleaning, send encouraging cards, help with day care if necessary, and provide flowers. Flowers are a huge asset. The majority of all women and their families have shared that the flowers were a big success and a great encouragement and comfort during their journey. Being on the giving side for many years, it was absolutely the most wonderful experience to be truly on the receiving end in so many ways. The flowers are one of everybody's favorite sources of encouragement and inspiration. Joan's husband donated to our memorial and shared how much his wife truly enjoyed the flowers. Amy's husband and family not only donated after her memorial, they still actively continue to support the foundation.

Speaking from my own experience and that of others, the chemo has so many side effects. You have mouth sores, no appetite, food limitations, reactions to certain foods, and reactions to smells, even cooking or fragrant perfumes or candles. You could read some but not a whole lot, having watery eyes and headaches. The flowers were and still are one of the biggest influences and inspiration of comfort to women and their families going through breast cancer. I truly believe the reason why our support group gets such high regard is because the group is supported by real cancer survivors and because we can share and relate to our common experience; we have compassion and understanding and can encourage other women with a genuine concern, which has positive results.

I would love to see other breast cancer survivors buddy up with someone that has been newly diagnosed; they will become "Breast Friends" with such a deeper level of friendship. As a Breast Friend as you can make a difference in this world in somebody else's life, by helping others to get through life's challenges. Breast cancer is not just a physical cancer; it is an emotional battle too. I am so very thankful for each and every one who helped me in any way on my journey. If I can make a positive difference for even one person, then my life is making a difference. If you would like to help women diagnosed with breast cancer you may visit our website at www.bfcancersupportgroup.org.

I Saw God Today

"I saw God today" in the flowers. "I saw God today" in the rising of the sun, in the splendor of the sun setting. "I saw God today" in the love that was shared in the loss of a loved one. "I saw God today" with the mending of marriages and broken relationships, saving children's hope and homes from the catastrophic consequences of divorce. "I saw God today" in the marriages of two lives being united. "I saw God today" in the forgiveness between parents and children, forgiveness in friendships and with the broken. "I saw God today" in the random act of kindness. "I saw God today" in the tears and the joy of being touched with the gift of flowers. His fingerprints were all over it. "I saw God's love touch someone's life today." "I saw God today" in the morning glory and felt His presence in the garden. "I saw God today" when the deaf heard the silent language of love. "I saw God today" when the blind could see the beauty through the senses of smell and was touched through the heart. I saw God Today and felt the love, as the tears welled through the blindness of the darkened eyes. "I saw God today" touch someone's soul. "I saw God today" in the birth of a new baby. "I saw God today" when He picked someone to go home. "I saw God today" by the ocean, in a field, on the plains, from the mountaintop, in the meadow, on the streets in the city, on a beach, on the bench in a park, on the path during my walk. "I saw God today."

Have you seen God today? Let God's love flow through you like a stream flowing to the river, rushing to the ocean of love.

Be a vessel that God can flow through and rain His blessings around you; then you will see God today. You will feel His presence. Look around; can you see God today? Do you hear the whisper of the silent language of love? Do you feel the warmth of the sun? Do you hear the leaves rustling in the gentle breeze? Do you hear the refreshing water in the stream? Do you see the splendor of the beauty around you? If you do, you are alive. Yes, you are alive. You are no different than the grain of sand, vapor in the wind, leaf on a tree, petal of a flower, grape on the vine, drop of rain in the ocean—you are alive with every breath you take; let God's love flow through you like a river deep and wide. Bring life to the dying and see, there's life in everything. I saw God today. Did you?

We often think that God is in the grand forces like the thunder; however, God's ways are not always highly visible. In fact, He often shows himself in the subtle ways or sometimes He chooses to come in a soft, gentle whisper. We all have jobs, a purpose, a gift, a talent, a reason for our own lives. We are all unique and special in our own way. We are made in the image of God, and we can all be great at what we do. We are teachers, nurses, doctors, farmers, florists, carpenters, singers, dancers, entertainers, beauticians, cooks, artists, etc. Yet we all can be great at what we do.

We all have the opportunity to be used by God to be a blessing to someone else. We all have a big job to do and to be. God uses the hands and skills of doctors and nurses to help heal the sick. We can all be used like Jesus. We can be the hands or the feet of God. It does not take a Master's degree to love one another; we can be masters at loving God, ourselves and others.

We really could bring a little more of heaven here on earth with all the beautiful flowers of gardens. All the love shared between one another would be so pleasing to our heavenly father.

Can one possibly even imagine what heaven could be like? Heaven is where life never ends, flowers and roses never fade and beautiful gardens of flowers are everywhere. In heaven there is always the fresh aroma of spring rains and fresh flowers, and love growing everywhere all the time.

As the sun is to the flowers, so is the Son to the soul. Find your sun (Son). Bloom where God plants you. Enjoy every minute of life, living in the moment. I encourage you to stop and smell the flowers along the way and hope you will see the real beauty within each and every one.

Raise the Bar

What type of legacy and living will are you creating now? A definition of a legacy is someone's lasting contribution to the world, to society or to his family. It may include money, but in many cases, it's more of a by-product of an individual's life. Your legacy is a result of what you have focused on in your life and is the expression (in terms of action) of your primary message.

We all begin life at birth, and all roads lead to a final rendezvous; the difference is what we do en route. Paths chosen, actions taken and a host of decisions made may lead ultimately to a unique legacy. It's non-negotiable: You will leave a legacy. The question is not whether you'll leave a legacy but what legacy you will leave. Your legacy comprises both ends and means. Is winning really winning when you are ashamed of how victory came? The means by which you move through your life provides the working platform that supports your goals.

Character style, courtesy, honesty, respect, giving, serving, integrity, love and caring—these are the qualities that make for an inspiring legacy. The way you live your life has an effect on how you are remembered. How can the ends of your efforts be respected if the means make you want to blush in embarrassment? Often when we think about a legacy, we consider it to be something that is left behind after a person has passed. A living legacy has the power to spur you on to live a mindful and proactive life. Every single one of us leaves a legacy. Your very existence has an impact on the world whether you intend it or not. Ask yourself, "If I died today…"

- What would I want people to say about me?
- How have I helped other people?
- Have I done my best, given my all?
- Did my life have meaning and purpose?
- Did I make a difference?
- Have I enhanced God's Kingdom?

Working toward a legacy in both your business and personal life keeps you motivated and performing at your peak. It gives a higher purpose to your life and work. Your work has an edge and energy because you're no longer just "doing work"; you're building a legacy. Above all, it helps you share the fullest of what you are. That's what I call success!

Inherently, individuals have a desire to leave something special behind to mark the value and purpose of their life. Not just a bequest to a cause, but rather a combination of a life of dedication and focus that results in a ripple effect that positively impacts society, whether in the community, globally or in the family. Do more things that will live on after you're gone. This gives purpose, passion and meaning to your life.

Write to leave a legacy. We often read about a financial legacy. There are advisors who can help you determine your goals and make sure that you have adequate money to achieve them. You are asked if you want to leave money to your children, to your church, to your college or high school, to a favorite charity.

Live your life as a legacy for your family and friends. Consider the variety of elements of your life that you want to include. Often the success story of a life of relationships is more valuable than a check or other monetary asset. Your children, grandchildren, great grandchildren, etc. can know what your life was like, what was important to you and what times were like when you lived. As a commercial might say, "Priceless." Start living today; don't wait to realize when you're dead that you haven't lived. Always be grateful for what you have right now. Live life as if you were dying.

Life Sentence

People will summarize your life in one sentence. What will that be? What would you do differently?

What if I had done more things of real value? What if I reflected more? What if I risked more? What if I gave generously? What if I loved more intensely? Did I live faithfully? Did I live fully? When was the last time I said thank you? Did I serve others joyfully? Did I care deeply? Did I speak kindly and encourage others? Did I make a difference to someone else today? Did I encourage or uplift another in some way? Did I share God's word with anyone at all? Did I obey His direction or answer the call? Did I love, forgive, help or show grace in any way? Could Christ be seen in my heart, my face, my actions or my response? Did I make a difference to someone else today? I pray that I will do, am doing, and have done His will, His way.

I expect to only pass through this world but one time, so any good thing that I can do, or any act of kindness that I can show to any fellow creature, let me do it now, in my time. Let me not procrastinate or find something else to do. Let me not defer or neglect to do or be what I'm supposed to do and be, for I shall not pass this way again. I want my life to reflect how I want to treat others and how I want to be treated. Let me not take one blessing for granted or waste my precious time on this earth on frivolous, unimportant things.

I will only pass through this world but once, and I want what I do to truly matter to God and others. I want to share the gospel to further his Kingdom, by planting seed of faith, hope and love. I want to make a difference in the world today. This is my daily prayer for me and for you. When you were born, you cried, and the world rejoiced on that day. I want to encourage you to live your life in such a way that when you die, the world cries while you rejoice. Live life fully and faithfully, as though you were dying. Every day is a gift with a bow wrapped around you, and you are the present (the gift) to the world.

May God's love and grace touch your heart with a beautiful garden of flowers. I pray in Jesus name,

Amen

A Note from the Author

A blessing is a greater blessing when it is shared with others. Please share your favorite story or many favorite stories of the expression of love. There is a story in each and every one of us. If you can't share it with me, please share your story with someone else today in a conversation with a stranger or a loved one. You never know the impact it could have in changing someone else's life. We all need to love, support, and give encouragement to one another. Everyone at every age needs a flower.

If you have been touched in some way or have seen what flowers have done for people, I would love to hear about it. Please share your story or someone else's with me. I would love to do a sequel of other stories or moments when flowers whispered to you or others. Your story can help inspire others or change their perspective of flowers. Love is the greatest blessing, and it needs to be shared.

Share your story with me by mailing it to:

Flowers Whisper

P.O. Box 294

Windsor, CO 80550

www.debbie@debbiemartins.com